DRAMA SAMP

Preparations and Presentations for First Examinations

Andy Kempe

Blackwell Education

© Andy Kempe 1988

First published 1988   Reprinted 1990

Published by Basil Blackwell Ltd
108 Cowley Road
Oxford OX4 1JF
England

Typeset by Columns of Reading   Printed in Great Britain

British Library Cataloguing in Publication Data

Drama sampler: preparations and presentations
   for first examinations
   1. Drama in English, 1558–1980–Anthologies –
   For schools
   I. Kempe, Andy
   882'.008

   ISBN 0–631–90277–5

The author and publishers wish to make the following acknowledgements

Reproduced by permission of Methuen London Ltd:
   The Body by Nick Darke
   Example by the Belgrade TIE Company, from *Theatre-in-Education Programmes: Secondary*, Ed. Pam Schweitzer
   Indians by Arthur Kopit
   The Lucky Ones by Tony Marchant
   She's Dead from *Tests* by Paul Abelman
   Vinegar Tom by Caryl Churchill, from *Plays by Women: Volume One*, Ed. by Micheline Wandor
Gregory's Girl by Bill Forsyth, reproduced by permission of the Cambridge University Press
Candleford by Keith Dewhurst, reproduced by permission of Century Hutchinson Ltd
The Golden Pathway Annual © 1975 by John Harding and John Burrows (Copyright agent Michael Imison Playwrights 28 Almeida St. London N1 1TD)
The Wild Duck by Henrik Ibsen, from *Hedda Gabler and other plays*, 1961, translated by Una Ellis-Fermor © the Estate of Una Ellis-Fermor, 1950, reproduced by permission of Penguin Books Ltd
A Dream Play by August Strindberg, reproduced by permission of Secker and Warburg
Johnson over Jordan by J.B. Priestley, reprinted by permission of A.D. Peters & Co Ltd

Contents

The number in brackets after each play denotes the
number of speaking parts in the extract.

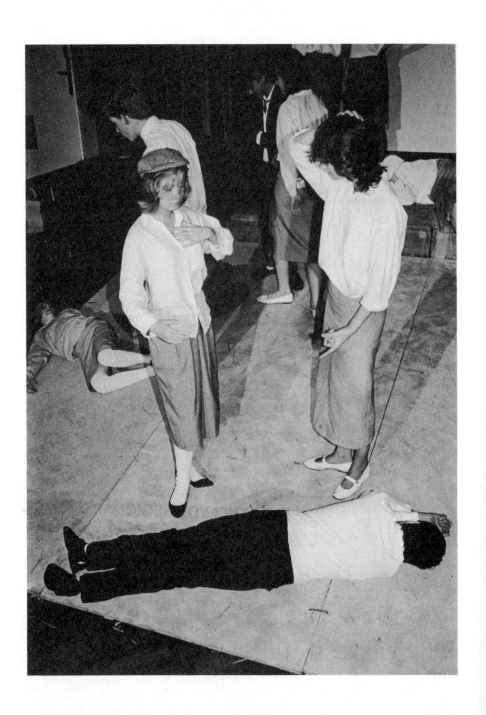

Preface

One of the most time-consuming and frustrating parts of teaching Drama and Theatre Arts is when students say, 'We want a play to do.' It seems like an innocent enough expression of interest but can pose sizeable problems for teachers regardless of their age, experience and bookstock. What if

- The store cupboard is bare/outdated/inaccessible?
- There is no money to buy either whole new sets or even samples of a wide range of plays?
- The lack of storage space means that the thought of students rummaging through the crammed cupboard gives you a headache?
- The county library is miles away and you can't take out all the plays you need anyway?

If you are new to Drama teaching you may feel unsure about what will go down well with your group. You may be uncertain about what the range of suitable plays is.

You may be an experienced teacher but suffer from 'idea auto-replay syndrome', so that when students ask you to suggest a play you always find yourself recalling the same ones.

The fact that you are a Drama teacher probably means that you have very little time to read or see new plays.

Another problem the teacher must face is that when students ask for a play they very often don't need a full-length script but just an extract long enough to experiment with or perhaps present. Even if teachers were able to carry catalogues of plays around in their already overloaded heads, it's a tall order to expect them to be able to cross-reference their casts, subject matter, genre, difficulties of style and language and then be able to assist different groups tackling all these different plays and develop the ideas arising from them. It's equally daunting for the students to be given a full-length play to share between four or five and be told, 'Here you are. You should be able to find something in this to suit you'.

This anthology won't solve all the problems you experience in looking for plays for use at first examination level, but I hope it will give the flavour of a number of plays you may not have considered before and some fresh ideas for exploring them. Some of the practical suggestions are deliberately designed to allow the teacher and the students to work together as a whole class. In fact, whilst the students should be able to tackle most of the work in their own groups, the questions are there as an aid to learning rather than a test. If you, the teacher, can provide further guidance without dictating the outcome of the work, then so much the better – what they can do with your help today they will do on their own tomorrow.

Andy Kempe

Note: Throughout this book the pronoun 'she' is used. This does not mean that I think only girls do drama: it's easier to read than 'he/she' or 's/he'!

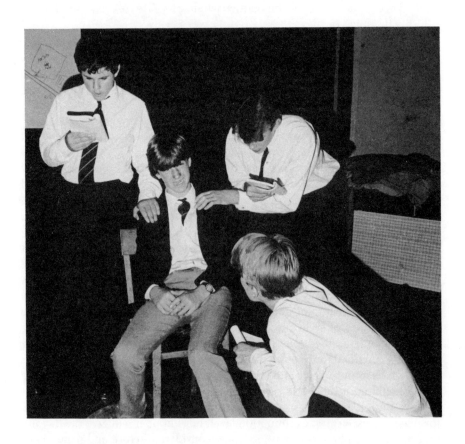

Introduction

Record companies used occasionally to produce albums called 'samplers'. They were a collection of tracks from new albums released on that label. The idea was that you could buy the sampler quite cheaply and experience a range of music; if there were any tracks you particularly liked you might go out and buy the whole of that album. It certainly worked in my case and I don't see why other art forms shouldn't use the same device.

This collection of extracts takes plays from a wide range of periods and styles. Though it's not a book on theatre history, the placing of each extract in a broad historical perspective may help you see a little more clearly both what the playwright is trying to do, and why. The extracts are separated into five different categories according to the sort of emotional reaction they might produce. Of course very few plays fit neatly into just one pigeon-hole and one might say that the best theatre is that which provokes a whole range of contrasting emotions. The categories are simply a guide or starting point.

Each extract should last between 10 and 20 minutes if staged. The exercises which follow are divided into three sections, all of which offer opportunities for discussion, and for practical or written work. The first section attempts to guide you towards a better understanding of the extract: who's who, what's going on and why. The second section asks a number of theatrical questions which will remind you that plays are written to be staged, and that their visual impact is often just as important as what the characters are actually saying. Finally, there are some suggestions as to how the themes, style or characters can be developed to create work of your own.

Just as record companies hoped that selling samplers would make people buy whole albums, I would hope that some, if not most, of these extracts will make you want to see or read the rest of the play. If, for the time being, you just need to work on one of these extracts – either to present it as it stands or use as the basis for a piece of work devised by yourselves – here are some guidelines that will help you avoid the common pitfalls of this type of project. They are certainly not the only means of tackling a presentation and your own teacher will often be able to help you more quickly and effectively. But you can refer back to them throughout your project and use them as a checklist of things you have or haven't done.

INTRODUCTION

Presenting a piece of scripted theatre

To get from the initial idea of presenting a play to actually putting it on in front of an audience can be like fighting your way through a jungle. Where do you start? Where do you go next?

What follows in this section is a possible route.

To sort out a muddle you need to put your demands into an order:

We need to like what we're doing.
We'll have to agree about what we like.

↓

We'll have to be able to work as a group
and talk to each other.

↓

Just talking can be dull.
We'll need to get into action as soon as possible.

↓

We won't know the words but we can use our own ideas
to keep the scene going.

↓

We'll need to decide who's going to watch the play, and
remember them as we decide how to play the scene.

↓

We're pressed for time and probably lack technical experience.
We'll have to keep it simple.

↓

If we're doing a scripted play we'll need
to learn the lines and get rid of the books.

↓

It's going to be hard but we mustn't give up.
We'll have to keep using our own ideas to solve the problems.

↓

We'll need to have everything ready before showing it. We'll need to
know all the lines, know where to stand, have the right costumes, the
right props and know what to do with them.

↓

We'll need to rehearse it as if an audience is really there.
We'll need to have a dress rehearsal which is as much like a real
performance of the play as possible.

↓

When we've done it, we'll need to know where
and why it worked or failed.
We'll need to be able to build on our strengths.

INTRODUCTION

1 Choose what you like best

● Don't simply decide to tackle a script because it's the first one that turns up. The most important thing a script must do is interest you. If it does this you will feel keener to work out the problems involved in staging it. Getting hold of and reading a copy of the whole play, or better still seeing it, will help you enormously in your own work.

● Students often pick a play simply because the number of people in their group matches the number in the cast. This isn't a good way of approaching the problem. It would be better to find a play you like and try to persuade people to be in it by explaining why you think it's worth doing.

2 Work as a group

● Everyone in the group must read through the extract – if not the whole play. If you try to take a back seat and just do what others tell you the whole project will quickly become very boring. If it is others in your group who aren't really involved try to encourage them rather than criticise them – it may be that they don't wholly understand the play and feel uncomfortable with it.

● Having found an extract which seems to interest the whole group, read it through at least three times. Change the casting each time and don't be deceived into thinking that the character who has least to say must be the easiest part – he/she may be on stage the whole time, in which case they will have to be doing something; at least when the playwright has written words for the part you have some idea of what you're meant to be doing.

3 Talk through the problems

● Having read the play make a few preliminary decisions on what it's about. The questions at the end of the extract will help you here, but before tackling them you could simply ask yourself the following questions:

> Who appears in this extract?
> Where is it set?
> When is it set?
> What is the tone/atmosphere of it?
> What actually happens?
> What sort of people are the characters?

4 Get into action

• Avoid getting into arguments about who is going to play who in the early stages. The main thing is to get the play off the page and into action so that you can see where the problems are and possibly discover who will be able to solve them best. You might, at this point, choose to have a director who will be able to tell you what the thing looks like and suggest ways of improving and developing it.
• After your initial readings, 'walk' through the play by setting up an area which is very roughly where you'd imagine the play to be set. Use chairs or, possibly, chalk marks on the floor to provide an outline.

5 Use your own ideas

• Put down the extracts and try to improvise the scene. Don't worry about getting the lines right – just try to include the major bits of the action and possibly a sense of what the characters are like.
• By improvising the scene like this three or four times you will begin to see how the characters relate to each other, what they think of each other and how they feel about the situation they are in. Test this against another reading of the script to see if your version of it is going in the right direction. If you have a director, she will be able to judge whether or not your improvised version really did resemble the original in any way.

6 Keep it moving

• If moving around the marked-out area seems difficult, try to act out the scene by having someone else read all the lines while you provide the actions. Without the book to distract you, you will be able to concentrate more both on your movements and facial expressions.

7 Who's going to watch?

• At this point you ought to remind yourselves that a play has an audience. With a lot of plays the audience watches from one direction only. If this is the case you will have to adjust the way you are positioned so that the audience always has a good view of what is most important. As a general rule the further 'upstage' you are (that is, the further you are from the audience) the closer to the centre line of the stage you should be. If you are 'downstage' and close to the audience when others are on stage, you should be out towards the edge of the stage. This isn't a hard and fast rule, but I suggest you use it as a basis and develop it into more interesting patterns if you can. Some plays don't require an audience to watch from just one direction: they might be all around the stage (look at *She's Dead*), or perhaps on two sides of it with the acting in a channel in the middle (look at *Example*). You must decide where the audience is going to be and rehearse with that in mind.

8 Keep it simple

● Don't waste time early on in rehearsals making scenery and props which will get broken or lost. The most important thing is to be able to tell the story and help the audience see what the characters are like. Sets are not as important as what happens on them, so if you are pressed for time, keep things as simple as you can.

● You might find that one or two props are very important to a character, in which case you should rehearse with them as much as possible. In *The Golden Pathway Annual*, for example, the Headmaster's cane is almost a part of the man himself, so the actor must feel used to having it in his hand. Similarly, a costume or, in the case of *Johnson Over Jordan*, a mask, can present big problems to an actor if he/she is not used to it.

9 Get rid of the books

● Some people can learn lines very quickly indeed. If you are one of these people, then you should start learning your lines straight away so that you can get rid of the book and concentrate on learning how to use your hands as part of the character. If you aren't so quick at learning lines you should still start trying to learn them immediately, as putting it off will only make you feel the pressure even more. Don't try to learn lines just by reading them through time and again. You really need to test yourself on them by turning the book over and trying to remember them. Better still is to get someone to help you by reading the other parts and stopping when it's your turn. Lines will only come across and sound natural if they are well learnt and you are used to saying them. Similarly, it's impossible to build a convincing picture on stage when everyone is holding a book.

10 Stick with it

● The worst thing you can do when working towards a presentation is to keep changing groups or to keep changing your minds about what play you want to do. Don't start rehearsing until you feel sure that you have chosen the right play and the right group. Once you've started then stick to your decision. All projects go through a rough patch when little progress seems to be made and you've said all the lines so many times they become boring. You just have to press on and rehearse it to the point when the material becomes effective again not for you but for someone who is watching it for the first time.

• Lights and sound effects will need to be added, but again, don't make your lives unnecessarily complicated by trying to do anything too complex. Much will, of course, depend on the equipment and experience you have available.

11 Tried and tested

• Before performing to an audience you should have a full dress rehearsal in which absolutely everything is as you want it. If a prop hasn't appeared at this stage you have no guarantee that it ever will. Treat the dress rehearsal as a performance.
• Tackling a piece of script isn't easy but is enormously rewarding if it is a piece that you personally enjoy and feel something for. If you rush your preparations or try to take short cuts you can end up hating what you once liked. Put your own ideas in and you'll end up liking it more.

12 Evaluate what you have done

• At the end of any performance you will no doubt have a 'gut' reaction as to how it went. Whilst not suggesting you ignore your own immediate feelings, you need to be able to nail down where those feelings are coming from. To go away saying 'It was great' or 'It was rubbish', will not help your future work unless you can identify just what was 'great' or 'rubbish' about it.
• Ask other people for their reactions to the work. Members of an audience will notice things you may have missed. What might be clear and satisfying to you may have confused and frustrated them. Did you really communicate what you wanted to communicate?
• Criticism is only useful if it is constructive. By being critical of yourself and accepting other people's assessment of your work you should feel better equipped and more confident about tackling future projects.

Building a play from improvisation

1 Start on firm ground

• Improvisations tend to fly off in unexpected directions once launched. The main thing is to launch them. If you can isolate, first of all, just one thing you want to concentrate on from the extract on which you are basing the improvisation, you will have a strong enough starting-point. Look at the following:

An attic room (*The Wild Duck*)
A dead body (*She's Dead*)
A condemned person (*Example*)
Two sides who can't understand each other (*Indians*)
Hiding your naughtiness (*The Country Wife*)
Daydream (*The Golden Pathway Annual*)
'I've been ill' (*Johnson Over Jordan*)

Any place, character, theme, line, incident or style can be used as a starting point.

2 *Don't talk, do*

● Actually improvising on your feet will generate many more ideas than sitting around discussing what you might do. The best ideas are often those produced spontaneously. Having agreed on a starting point, it should be easy to develop the improvisation from there.

Two people sit in an attic room. Someone walks in and . . .

A dead body lies on the ground. Into the scene walks . . .

It is the night before the execution. The condemned man . . .

If you have just finished any of the above sentences you already have the basis for your improvisation.

● Improvisations are all about trying to generate ideas, so don't worry about ending them. The end will be when it 'dries up'. At this point sit and remind yourself of the strong elements of what you have just created. It would be useful if you could write them down or record them for future reference.

3 *Develop a thread*

● It is very likely that in the course of one of your improvisations you will hit upon something that immediately strikes you as being worth further exploration. Alternatively, you may want to stick to some of the other ideas in the original extract. Either way, you need to develop your improvisations until you have plenty of material from which to build the scenes you eventually decide on.

● One way of doing this is simply to take a different perspective:

Two people sit in an attic room talking about someone. Suddenly that very person walks in . . .

You are passing a house and hear shouting coming from the attic room. You know the people in there so you . . .

You are the furniture in the attic room. If only you could talk you'd be able to tell of the time when . . .

● After improvising 'around' the situation in this way you may be able to see not only the drama in the original incident but how that situation developed and the implications of it for the future.

4 Make a treatment

● A 'treatment' is simply a brief incident-by-incident account of a story; it need be no more than a list of the major events of the play noting, for example, when people come in, when/why they leave, and their attitude towards and effect on the others in the scene. Your story might be told in a number of short scenes or through a number of key incidents within a longer scene. Writing or recording a simple treatment will serve as a good foundation when you go on to polish the work.

5 'Go for it'

● Improvisations can go on forever if you let them. If your task is to present a piece of theatre you will have to stop adding new material at some point and shape what you've already created. You might want to try to script what you've done, but often lines which were funny when spoken spontaneously sound awful when learnt as lines on a page. Try instead to work from your treatment so that an element of spontaneity is kept.
● Refer back to the suggestions for working from a script for ideas about when and how to tackle set, props, lights, sound and the final rehearsals.
● Finally, don't worry about improvisations 'going wrong'. Their strength as pieces of theatre is that they are new and alive and therefore prone to having good days and bad days. Just because your improvisation has a few bad days don't smother it – perhaps it just needs treating with a bit more care.

6 Evaluate

● The process of evaluation is as important here as for a piece of scripted work, though there is the possibility that you will feel more personally affected by it – these are, after all, your own ideas on the line. For this reason you should be clear that what is being assessed is not so much the quality of your original idea but how well it worked in performance.

THE WILD DUCK

by Henrik Ibsen

CAST (in order of appearance)

HJALMAR
GINA
GREGERS
HEDWIG

4 speaking parts. No doubling.

During the last century the theatre had, in many ways, fallen into the trap
of following formulas. Certain techniques and story-lines had been
discovered which, if used in an accepted, conventional way, would provide
the author with a sure-fire success. In Northern Europe, and most certainly
Britain, people had got used to watching melodramas which presented
them with stereotyped situations, characters and emotions. Whilst some of
these melodramas survive today, a great many do not because they are
simply not good enough. Ibsen was a Norwegian writer who wanted to
revive the theatre by using it to show people something about real life. He
often dealt with sensitive social issues and some people thought his work
shocking because of this. In many of his plays he takes a strongly
moralistic attitude and comments on subjects like divorce, venereal
disease, and corruption and greed amongst those in authority. (The film
Jaws is said by some to be a reworking of his play *An Enemy of the
People*.)

In *The Wild Duck*, Ibsen tells the story of one family being destroyed by
the influence of another. Werle is a wealthy local merchant who
commands respect with all except his son, Gregers. At some time in the
past Werle had a partner called Ekdal and the two of them were involved
in an illegal business deal. Werle somehow managed to escape the scandal,
but Ekdal lost all he had. Gregers suspects his father is to blame for
Ekdal's downfall and feels strongly that justice ought to be done. He sets
about trying to achieve this by renewing an old friendship with Ekdal's
son, but his presence simply stirs up old troubles. Ekdal and his

11

granddaughter keep a wild duck in the attic. It was shot by Werle and now just hangs on to life. The duck seems to *symbolise* (or represent) many themes in the play. Its presence in the Ekdal's attic could be said to represent the secrets from the past which the family wishes to keep hidden. In particular its wounded and vulnerable condition mirrors the situation of the granddaughter, Hedvig.

The style of the play

Ibsen felt that in order for his plays to make the points he wanted them to make, he would have to forget many of the theatrical conventions of the day and write lines that sounded natural and convincing. This was shocking to the audiences of the time because it wasn't what they were used to. Ibsen wanted people to believe in the situations and stories he was creating. His style of writing is often described as *naturalistic*; in other words, he tried to capture real dialogue in the same way that a hidden tape-recorder might record it. This style influenced many later writers, but whereas their work has not lasted, Ibsen's is still freqently produced. This may be partly because the themes and subjects which Ibsen deals with make his plays seem as relevant today as they did then.

The extract

Hedwig, Ekdal's granddaughter, is going blind. When Ekdal's son, Hjalmar, learns that Werle is also going blind he begins to suspect that his wife, who was once Werle's maid, has deceived him about whose daughter Hedvig really is. His suspicions are strengthened when a letter arrives from Werle saying that he intends to leave Hedwig some money. Hjalmar feels used and cheated. Gregers seems to think that it will be possible to wipe the slate clean. By pursuing a policy of openness and honesty and refusing to take Werle's money, old sins will be turned into moral strengths. Hjalmar's wife, Gina, has a more down-to-earth approach, however, and believes that the secrets of the past should be forgotten so that people can just get on with their lives. Werle is casting a shadow over the Ekdal family in a number of ways. He has affected old Ekdal, Hjalmar's wife Gina and, of course, Hedvig. In addition his son influences Hjalmar to the point where the family may be completely destroyed. Meanwhile, up in the attic, the wild duck that Werle shot but didn't kill lies in the semi-darkness waiting to die.

HJALMAR   I want to know whether – your child has the right to live under my roof.

GINA [*drawing herself up, with her eyes flashing*]   And you ask that?

HJALMAR   You're to answer this question. Does Hedvig belong   5
to me – or . . . Well?

GINA [*looking at him with cold defiance*]   I don't know.

HJALMAR [*trembling*]   You don't know that?

GINA   How can *I* know that? The sort of woman I am –

HJALMAR [*quietly, turning away from her*]   Then I have   10
nothing more to do in this house.

GINA   Think what you are doing, Hjalmar.

HJALMAR [*putting on his overcoat*]   There is nothing here to think about, for a man like me.

GREGERS   On the contrary, there is a very great deal to think   15
about. You three must be together if you are to win the great sacrament of forgiveness.

HJALMAR   That I will *not*. Never! Never! My hat! [*Picks it up.*]
My home has collapsed in ruins about me. [*Bursting into tears.*] Gregers! I have no child!   20

HEDVIG [*who has opened the kitchen door*]   What are you saying? [*Going across to him.*] Daddy, Daddy!

GINA   There, now!

HJALMAR   Don't come near me, Hedvig! Go away! Right away! I can't bear to look at you. Ah, the eyes! Good-bye.   25
[*Making towards the door.*]

HEDVIG [*clinging tightly to him and screaming*]   No, no! Don't go away from me!

GINA [*crying out*]   Look at the child, Hjalmar! Look at the child!   30

HJALMAR   I won't. I can't. I must get out, away from all this!

He tears himself free from HEDVIG *and goes out by the hall door.*

HEDVIG [*with despair in her eyes*)   He's going away from us, Mother! He's going away from us! He'll never come back again.

GINA   Don't cry, now, Hedvig. Father will come back again.   35

HEDVIG [*throwing herself down on the sofa, sobbing*] No, no, he'll never come back to us again.

GREGERS You do believe, Mrs Ekdal, that I meant it all for the best?

GINA Yes, I half believe you did; but God forgive you, all the same.

HEDVIG [*lying on the sofa*]. I think I'm going to die of all this. What have I done to him? Mother, you must make him come home again.

GINA Yes, yes. Just be quiet, and I'll go out and look for him. [*Putting on her outdoor coat.*] Perhaps he's gone down to Relling. But you mustn't lie there and cry, now. Will you promise me that?

HEDVIG [*sobbing convulsively*] Yes, I'll stop crying, if only Daddy comes back.

GREGERS [*to* GINA, *who is just going*] Wouldn't it be better, all the same, to let him fight his bitter fight to the end first?

GINA Oh, he can do that afterwards. First and foremost we must get the child quieted down. [*She goes out by the hall door.*]

HEDVIG [*sitting up and drying her tears*] Now you must tell me what is the matter. Why doesn't Daddy want to see me any more?

GREGERS You mustn't ask about that till you are big and grown-up.

HEDVIG [*with a sob*] But I can't go on being absolutely miserable till I'm big and grown-up. I think I know what it is. Perhaps I'm not Daddy's real child.

GREGERS [*uneasily*] How could that happen?

HEDVIG Mother may have found me. And now perhaps Daddy has found it out. I've read about that sort of thing.

GREGERS Well, but even so —

HEDVIG Yes, I think he must be just as fond of me, for all that. Almost more. The wild duck was sent us as a present, too; and I'm tremendously fond of that, just the same.

GREGERS [*distracting her attention*] Yes, the wild duck; that reminds me. Let's talk about the wild duck a little, Hedvig.

HEDVIG The poor wild duck! He can't bear to look at that any more, either. Just think, he wanted to wring its neck.

GREGERS Oh, he certainly won't.   75
HEDVIG No, but he said it. And I think it was dreadful of
  Daddy to say that. Because I say a prayer for the wild duck
  every night and ask that it shall be protected from death and
  everything bad.
GREGERS [*looking at her*] Do you say your prayers at night? 80
HEDVIG Of course.
GREGERS Who taught you?
HEDVIG I taught myself; because there was a time when
  Daddy was very ill and had leeches on his neck and said he
  was lying at death's door.   85
GREGERS What, really?
HEDVIG So I said a prayer for him, when I'd gone to bed. And
  I've gone on with it ever since.
GREGERS And now you pray for the wild duck, too?
HEDVIG I thought I'd better put in the wild duck, because she 90
  was so delicate at first.
GREGERS Do you say prayers in the morning, too?
HEDVIG Oh no, of course not.
GREGERS But why not in the morning, just as much?
HEDVIG Why, in the morning, it's light, and there is nothing 95
  to be afraid of any more.
GREGERS And the wild duck that you are so fond of – your
  father would like to wring its neck.
HEDVIG No, he said it would be best for him to, but he would
  spare it for my sake. And that was good of Daddy.   100
GREGERS [*coming a little nearer*] But suppose, now, that you,
  of your own free will, sacrificed the wild duck for *his* sake?
HEDVIG [*getting up*] The wild duck!
GREGERS Supposing that you were to give up, as a sacrifice to
  him, the most precious thing you have in the world?   105
HEDVIG Do you think that would help?
GREGERS Try it, Hedvig.
HEDVIG [*quietly, with shining eyes*] Yes, I will try it.
GREGERS Have you strength of mind enough, do you think?
HEDVIG I will ask Grandfather to shoot the wild duck for me. 110
GREGERS But not a word to your mother about this kind of
  thing.
HEDVIG Why not?

GREGERS She doesn't understand us.

HEDVIG The wild duck? I will try it first thing tomorrow. 115

[GINA *comes in from the hall door.*]

HEDVIG [*going to her*] Did you meet him, Mother?

GINA No, but I heard he'd been down there and had taken Relling with him.

GREGERS Are you sure of this?

GINA Yes, the porter's wife said so. Molvik had gone with 120 them too, she said.

GREGERS And that at this moment, when his spirit so sorely needs to fight in solitude!

GINA [*taking off her coat*] Yes, you never know where you are with men. Lord knows where Relling has carted him off 125 to. I ran over to Mrs Eriksen's, but they weren't there.

HEDVIG [*fighting with her tears*] Oh, suppose he never comes home any more!

GREGERS He'll come home again. I'm going to take a message to him tomorrow, and then you'll see how he'll come. You 130 can go to sleep and trust to that, Hedvig. Good night.

He goes out through the hall door.

HEDVIG [*throwing herself sobbing on her mother's neck*] Mother! Mother!

GINA [*patting her on the back and sighing*] Ah yes; Relling was right, he was. This is what happens when these fools of 135 people come around presenting these here 'Idol's claims'.

Understanding the text

1 Divide a piece of paper into two columns, heading one EKDAL and the other WERLE. Write down the names of all the characters in the appropriate columns, showing the relationship between them. Draw arrows between the two columns and write, along the line of the arrow, what the relationship is. For example, the arrow between Hjalmar Ekdal and Gregers Werle should read 'old friends'. (You will need to leave a lot of space between the names since the relationships are quite complex!)

2 Hjalmar and Gregers are meant to be old friends. Do you think Gregers is a good friend? What does Hjalmar's attitude to him seem to be?

3 How would you describe Gina's attitude towards Gregers? Bear in mind who he is and what his relationship to her family is. Does this explain her attitude in any way?

4 Pick out three lines which might suggest that Gregers is, in fact, the main cause of the problem in the Ekdal household.

5 Do you think Hedvig is treated well or shown respect by any of the characters in the scene? Pick out some lines from the extract to explain your opinion.

6 The play attempts to capture everyday language in Norway about 100 years ago. Pick out a few lines which you find rather unnatural and perhaps suggest alternatives. Try not to interfere with the atmosphere or characters of the original.

Producing the scene

1 In this scene it seems as if things are closing in on Hjalmar's family. The influence of Werle appears in Gregers, the letter and even the wild duck which he shot. Describe how you could suggest a sense of 'impending doom' either through set design or lighting.

2 Design or describe a costume that would suggest either Gregers's 'upright', moral attitude, or Hedwig's simple innocence.

3 The wild duck is never actually seen but nevertheless is of great importance in the play. How could you draw the audience's attention to its presence? Choose one or two moments in this scene when you might want to remind the audience in some way of its existence and experiment with practical ways of achieving this.

4 As Gregers is building up to suggesting that Hedvig kills the duck the audience might start to realise what he is up to. Work through this section in pairs and try to discover how movement, gesture and facial expression could be used to suggest what might be going to happen next in the play.

5 Make a list of all the differences between Gregers and Gina as characters. If you were directing this extract, how would you bring out these differences in the way the actors move and speak? Think, for example, of tone and volume of voice, whether or not they should look at each other or away from each other, and whether or not they should stand, sit, or walk around.

6 Divide into two groups of four. Choose a short section from the extract. Group A should read the characters' parts and watch as group B supply the appropriate actions. This technique can often illustrate effective ways of using facial expression and positioning in a scene. When you have gone through the scene, discuss what you have noticed and try it again.

Further development

1 In pairs, improvise a scene in which A feels she must be polite to B even though she personally dislikes B and thinks she is behaving wrongly.

2 For Hedvig to shoot the duck is a huge personal sacrifice. She thinks that doing it will help the family over its problems. In pairs, improvise a scene in which A tries to make B give up something personally valuable. Even though B tries to find an alternative A always manages to find another good reason.

3 Imagine that Hjalmar decides to divorce Gina because he has found out that Hedvig is not his true daughter. Prepare and improvise a scene in court in which Gina tries to explain why she did not tell Hjalmar the truth.

4 Gregers is an idealistic person and has very high expectations of Hjalmar. Earlier in the play his father, Werle, had warned him that Hjalmar is not as strong a man as Gregers thinks him to be. Invent a scene in which it is clear that one character (A) hero-worships another (B). A second scene should show how A is eventually brought back down to earth in her opinion of B.

5 Invent a scene in which the characters not only speak to each other, but also speak their thoughts aloud. For example:

WIFE You're late home, dear. (He's been to the pub!)

HUSBAND Yes. I was held up in the traffic. (I think I've got away with it)

WIFE Busy is it? (I'll catch him out)

HUSBAND Oh, you know, about the same as usual. (Maybe she suspects!) . . .

6 Choose a short section from the extract (the opening lines would be particularly suitable) and try to act it out in this way.

7 A similar technique to the one above which reveals what lies behind what a person says is not to say the line at all but just describe the nature of the statement or question. Use the same scene as the one you have invented for Question 5. For example:

WIFE Seemingly innocent question.

HUSBAND Cool answer.

WIFE Probe a bit deeper.

HUSBAND Careful evasion.

8 Try to represent, by use of movement only, the idea of a number of outside pressures building up on a person.

EXAMPLE

by the Belgrade TIE company

CAST (in order of appearance)

PETITIONER
PROCTOR
PASSER-BY
NARRATOR
SPOKESMAN (OFFSTAGE)
MRS BENTLEY
SILVERMAN
SPEAKER
DEREK BENTLEY

9 speaking parts. Doubling possible.

TIE stands for Theatre in Education. A great many schools now enjoy visits from TIE teams – perhaps your school is one of them. The aim of these teams of actor/teachers is to use theatre's ability to excite and involve young people to help them discover and understand something new.

Some TIE shows set up problems which require the audience to get actively involved in the finding of a solution. Others present a play which needs discussion and perhaps further research and practical work in order to understand the issues involved.

One such play is *Example*. It is the true story of Derek Bentley, who was hanged in 1953. Bentley had been involved in an attempted burglary with another boy, Christopher Craig, when they were apprehended by the police. Trapped on the roof of a warehouse Craig shot dead a police officer. The penalty for murder at the time was death by hanging. However, Craig was only 16 years old and too young to hang. Bentley, on the other hand, was 19, and although he was clearly not the murderer himself, the law judged that being older he was equally responsible.

The case caused a public uproar, particularly in the light of evidence that suggested that Bentley had limited intelligence and had, in fact, given himself up to the police before the shooting took place. Despite all this the judges felt it necessary to make an example of someone. The play looks into the reasons why they felt this way, but suggests strongly that hanging Bentley was not a satisfactory solution.

EXAMPLE

The style of the play

The play is presented in short, episodic scenes, starting with a look at the life and character of Derek Bentley. Time is telescoped so that the opening scenes cover a span of years, whereas the later ones trace the events in the last weeks and then, finally, the last hours of Bentley's life. This technique gives the play a growing sense of urgency which should be reflected in the way it is presented.

The characters are mostly real people, but nevertheless seem to represent certain viewpoints. A problem in staging the play is to make these firm views come across without stereotyping the characters into 'goodies' and 'baddies'.

The extract

The last few scenes of the play are presented here. Bentley has been sentenced and his appeal has been refused. The tension mounts as every effort is made to spare his life. This tension is enhanced theatrically by the shortness and sharpness of the scenes.

Scene six

> *The* PETITIONER *enters, holding copies of the petition. She talks to the audience.*

PETITIONER   I've got here a petition for the reprieve of Derek Bentley. I've got nearly 100,000 signatures and need more. Will you read the petition and if you agree with it, please sign.

> *She hands them out to the audience, then sees* PROCTER.

PETITIONER   Will you sign this, sir?   5
PROCTER [*looking at a copy*]   Petition for the reprieve of Derek Bentley. Very interesting. Having any success with it?
PETITIONER   Most people sign. I reckon we'll get over 100,000 signatures.
PROCTER   100,000 eh? Not bad. [*She continues with handing*   10
   out.] Er excuse me – are all these people against hanging?
PETITIONER   No, not all.

20

PROCTER   Just against hanging Derek Bentley?

PETITIONER   That's right.

PROCTER   Just a moment. One more thing – when you get all 15
these signatures you're going to take them to the Home
Secretary I presume?

PETITIONER   Yes, of course. He's the only one who can pardon
Bentley now. Excuse me.

> The PASSER-BY *enters.*

Excuse me, sir, will you sign the petition for the reprieve of 20
Derek Bentley?

PASSER-BY   Sorry, no.

> *He starts to move off.*

PROCTER   Could you tell me why you haven't signed the
petition?

PASSER-BY   Who are you?   25

PROCTER   [*producing press card*] Harry Procter, Sunday
Pictorial.

PETITIONER   [*to* PROCTER] If you're not going to sign the
petition can I have it back as there are people here who'll
sign.   30

PROCTER   Look, love, I'm trying to conduct an interview here.
Are you blind? [*To* PASSER-BY.] Sorry about that, sir. Now,
could you tell me why you didn't sign the petition?

PASSER-BY   I think it's a lot of fuss over nothing. If everybody
goes mad with petitions every time some young thug gets 35
sentenced to death, how will our police be safe?

PROCTER   So you think it's not fair to the police?

PASSER-BY   Very strongly. Who's thinking about the poor
widow of the policeman now? Who's making a fuss about
her? £2.16 a week pension that's all she gets. That'd be 40
worth getting up a petition about.

PETITIONER   I agree but –

PASSER-BY   But the real question is, can we really ask the police
to risk their lives on our behalf if they don't feel they're
supported by everybody and specially protected if things go 45
wrong. That's the main point. How do you think they'll feel
if this Bentley boy gets off?

PETITIONER But –

PASSER-BY [*to* PETITIONER] I'm sorry but your petition's a
  complete waste of time.   50

>   *He goes.*

PETITIONER [*calling after him*] But Mrs Miles herself thinks
  Bentley should be reprieved.

PROCTER [*to audience*] Oh, yeah, did you hear about that?
  Touching little scene it was. Policeman's Widow Says
  Bentley Should Not Hang. I mean, not quite page one but 55
  pretty strong for page two.

PETITIONER Look, are you going to sign or not?

PROCTER (*handing it back*] I don't think I'll bother. I mean
  the Press should remain impartial after all. And I mean,
  you've got more than enough signatures for the Home 60
  Secretary.

>   *The* PETITIONER *has collected in the petitions during this.*

PROCTER Do you mind if I come along to take a picture of
  your handing in the petition?

PETITIONER If you must.

>   *Slide of* MAXWELL-FYFE, *Home Secretary.*

NARRATOR Sir David Maxwell-Fyfe, Home Secretary.   65

PETITIONER We would like to present a petition on behalf of
  Derek William Bentley at present under sentence of death.

>   *A hand appears to receive the petition from her.* PROCTER
>   *takes photo.*

SPOKESMAN [*off*] The Home Secretary will give your petition
  due consideration. The parents of the prisoner will be
  informed of his decision in due course. [*The* PETITIONER *tries to* 70
  speak.] That is all.

PROCTER Thanks for the pic, mate. Don't reckon much to
  your chances though.

PETITIONER Oh really?

PROCTER Yes, really. I mean Maxwell-Fyfe's not only the 75
  Home Secretary, but he's also the head of the Police Force
  and it was a policeman that got it wasn't it?

PETITIONER   Why don't you shut up, you parasite?

She goes. PROCTER *laughs.*

PROCTER   Well, we'll wait and see, won't we.

The slide of MAXWELL-FYFE *stays. The sound of heartbeats is heard.* PROCTER *counts on his fingers, occasionally glancing at the slide of* MAXWELL-FYFE.

PROCTER   Fifteen days to go   80
  fourteen days to go
  thirteen days to go
  twelve days to go
  eleven days to go
  ten days to go   85
  nine days to go
  eight days to go
  seven days to go
  six days to go
  five days to go   90
  four days to go
  three days to go
  two days to go . . .

Scene seven

The slide and heartbeats fade. MRS BENTLEY *enters.* PROCTER *crosses to her.*

PROCTER   Mrs Bentley, Mrs Bentley, is it true the Home
  Secretary's rejected the petition?   95
MRS B   Rejected it?
PROCTER   You've heard nothing, Mrs Bentley?
MRS B   No, nothing. We're still waiting.
PROCTER   Oh.
MRS B   Why, what have you heard?   100
PROCTER   You've not had any word then?
MRS B   No messenger's been, nothing.
PROCTER   You've not had a letter, have you?

MRS B   Letter! . . . You'd better come in. The house is full of
letters but surely . . .   105
PROCTER   Perhaps you'd better take a look through them,
Mrs Bentley.
MRS B   But surely . . .
PROCTER   An official-looking envelope, Mrs Bentley, are you
sure you haven't seen one?   110
MRS B   But surely they wouldn't send it by ordinary post. They
couldn't leave us waiting.
PROCTER   Take a look, Mrs Bentley.

> *She brings out a large basket filled with letters. She
> empties it on the ground and starts searching through,
> eventually she finds the envelope. She opens it and starts
> to read.*

PROCTER   Is that it, Mrs Bentley? What does it say?

> *She stays kneeling silent and broken.*

Look up, Mrs Bentley.   115

> *She looks up. He takes a photo.* PROCTER *leaves. The
> heartbeats start up again. The mother stays on her knees.*

Scene eight

SILVERMAN [*as he enters*]   Mrs Bentley, Mrs Bentley –

> *Slide of* SILVERMAN. *He goes to* MRS BENTLEY *and during
> the following, helps her up.*

SILVERMAN   My name's Silverman. I'm an M.P. Some of us
have heard about your son's case and want to do something
about it.
MRS B   But the Home Secretary –   120
SILVERMAN   We're going to force a debate in the House of
Commons tonight. There are important factors that weren't
taken into account at the trial, factors such as your son's
epilepsy and his low I.Q. He must be reprieved. Will you
come?   125

Pause.

MRS B   Yes, of course.

They cross the stage. Heartbeats again.

Scene nine

Sound of general hubbub. Slide: 'The Commons Debate 27th January 1953, evening.' SILVERMAN *shows* MRS BENTLEY *to a seat.*

SILVERMAN   Sit there, Mrs Bentley, in the public gallery.
SPEAKER [*tape*]   Order! Order!

Fade hubbub as SILVERMAN *starts.*

SILVERMAN   Mr Speaker! Mr Speaker, yesterday shortly after 7.00 p.m. I presented for debate the motion 'that this House   130
does not agree with the Home Secretary's decision that there are not sufficient reasons for reprieving Derek Bentley, and urges him to reconsider the matter so far as to give effect to the recommendation of the jury and to the expressed view of the Lord Chief Justice that Bentley's guilt was less than that   135
of his co-defendant, Christopher Craig.' I have since been told by 'phone that on your instructions, the motion has been removed from the order paper. Is the House to wait until Bentley is dead before it is entitled to say he should not die?   140
SPEAKER [*tape*]   In this case the motion of the honourable member which I saw last night dealt with the case of a capital sentence which is still pending and there is a long line of authorities of all my predecessors saying that, if a capital sentence is pending, the matter shall not be discussed by the   145
House.
SILVERMAN   Mr Speaker, this is a matter which arouses interest of the deepest kind not merely in the House. I venture to think that if it were possible to put such a matter to the vote today, there would be an overwhelming majority of this   150
House who think that the Home Secretary has decided

wrongly. I have here more than 200 telegrams from all sorts of people all over the country, all of them except one holding the decision to be wrong, and that one telling me to mind my own business. Sir, I *am* minding my own business! That is why I am raising this question with you. It is the business of all of us if this boy is hanged when we think he ought not to be hanged. This is a parliamentary democracy and we are all responsible for what occurs.

SPEAKER [*tape*]   A motion can be put down on this subject when the sentence has been executed, the Minister responsible may be criticised on the relevant vote of Supply or on the Adjournment. I have stated that this is the practice of the House and I cannot alter the practice of the House.

SILVERMAN   A three-quarter witted boy is to be hanged for a murder that he did not commit and which was committed fifteen minutes after he was arrested. Can we be made to keep silent when a thing as horrible and shocking as this is to happen?

SPEAKER [*tape*]   I repeat that no debate on the subject can be held here until the execution has taken place. Only then can the justice of that execution be debated. That is my ruling based on all available Parliamentary precedent.

Blank slide. Pause. SILVERMAN *returns to where* MRS BENTLEY *sits silently.*

SILVERMAN   I'm sorry, Mrs Bentley.

MRS B   That's it then.

SILVERMAN   By no means, Mrs Bentley, don't give up now. A group of us are going to go to the Home Secretary's house tonight to argue with him face to face. We have signatures from 200 M.P.s. He must listen to us. [*Pause.*] I think you should go to your son, Mrs Bentley.

Pause.

MRS B   Yes.

SILVERMAN   We'll save him, Mrs Bentley. The Home Secretary will listen. Go and see Derek.

Both leave. The heartbeats again. Silence.

155

160

165

170

175

180

Scene ten

Sound of crowd noises. PROCTER *dashes on and goes to the phone.*

PROCTER The time 8.50 a.m. the 28th January, 1953, and only ten minutes to go before Derek Bentley is due to be 185
executed. Outside Wandsworth Prison a large and angry crowd has gathered to protest. The chants of 'Murder . . . murder' changed to cheers a few moments ago when a telegram boy arrived but it was a false alarm. He was not bringing Derek Bentley's reprieve. Even now extra squads of 190
police are standing by in case the crowd breaks into the prison to try to save Bentley. With only minutes to go now, the crowd has grown strangely quiet but no-one is leaving. The life of Derek William Bentley now hangs on the thin thread of a last minute change of heart by the Home 195
Secretary who appears to have ignored the deputation of M.P.s. Meanwhile, inside the prison, Derek William Bentley dictates his last letter . . .

PROCTER *puts down the receiver and goes. Silence.*

Scene eleven

BENTLEY *enters.*

BENTLEY Dear Mum and Dad, I was so glad to see you on my visit today. I got the rosary and the letter and I saw the 200
photo of the dog. Iris looked nice surrounded by all those animals. I could not keep the photo because it was a newspaper cutting. I told you, Mum, it would be very difficult to write this letter. I can't think of anything to say except you have all been wonderful the way you worked for 205
me. Don't forget what I told you, 'Always keep your chin up,' and tell Pop not to grind his teeth. I hope Dad has more televisions in. Oh, I forgot to ask him how things were on the visit. Oh, Dad, don't let my cycle frames get rusty because they might come in handy one day and, Dad, keep a 210
strict eye on Denis if he does anything wrong, though I don't

think he will, but you never know how little things can get you into trouble. If he does, wallop him so that he won't sit down for three weeks. I am trying to give you good advice because of my experience. I tell you, Mum, the truth of this story has got to come out one day and as I said in the visiting box, one day a lot of people are going to get into trouble and I think you know who those people are. What do you think, Mum? This letter may sound a bit solemn but I am still keeping my chin up as I want all the family to do. Don't let anything happen to the dogs and cats and look after them as you always have. I hope Laurie and Iris get married alright, I'd like to give them my blessing, it would be nice to have a brother-in-law like him. Laurie and I used to have some fun up at the pond till four o'clock in the morning, by the cafe. I always caught Laurie to pay for the pies, he never caught me. That will be all for now. I will sign this myself. Lots of love, Derek.

The heartbeats start up. BENTLEY *leaves. The heartbeats gradually fade. Pause. Enter* NARRATOR.

NARRATOR   Derek Bentley was hanged for the murder of P.C. Miles 28th January, 1953.

She leaves.

Understanding the text

1 One of the problems of any play, but perhaps TIE plays in particular, is to get information over to the audience so they can understand more clearly what is going on. Divide a sheet of paper into two columns and head them LINES and TECHNIQUES. Look at Scene Six and pick out all the lines and theatrical techniques that provide the audience with essential factual information. For instance, the Petitioner gets information across at the start of Scene Six by talking directly to the audience. Note the lines and techniques in the appropriate columns.
2 Procter appears in three of these scenes.
   • What sort of person do you think the writers want us to think he is?
   • Read through his lines again. What other special function does he appear to have?

3 Look at the last two scenes and read them aloud.
- What happens to the pace of the play here and how is this done?
- What effect does this have on the reader or audience?

4 What different viewpoints on the Bentley case are put forward in these last few scenes?
- Do you think the authors want you to think in a particular way about this case?
- Which arguments do you find particularly convincing?

Producing the scene

1 Note down the different locations for each scene. Devise a way of being able to move from one scene to another quickly so as not to break the mounting tension. Using spotlights on different areas would be one possible method, but if you use this technique you willl need to consider appropriate colours, angles and intensities, and the spread of each area. Note down any other methods of dividing up the acting area which might be useful here.

2 *Example* may well be more effective if performed 'in the round', that is, with the audience sitting all around the acting area. What would be the advantages and problems of using such a technique for this extract?

3 List the sound effects specified in the extract. Discuss the effect of the heartbeats and of having the voice of the Speaker on tape.

4 The stage directions suggest using slides at various places in the scene. What do you think the aim of this is and where could you position a screen on the stage to achieve this most effectively?

5 In performance *Example* tends to have a very emotional effect on an audience. One of the most touching moments is when Mrs Bentley finds the letter rejecting the petition and Procter tricks her into looking up so he can take a photograph of her crying. Rehearse this scene carefully and decide how best to change the pace in order to gain the most effect.

6 Read through the extract again, noting where and how tension is increased or lowered. Draw a graph to show how the pace of the extract varies. The horizontal axis should represent an approximate time scale (measured in key events and scenes) and the vertical axis should show the degree of tension and excitement. Label the points of highest tension which would excite an audience and also the 'troughs' where an audience is made to consider a line or effect more carefully.

Further development

1 A lot of the theatrical strength of *Example* comes from the way in which it changes the pace to capture and intensify emotional moments. Improvise a scene in which two or three people are enjoying themselves but then something happens which suddenly changes the atmosphere.

2 The Press are often criticised for the way they probe into personal tragedies in order to get their stories. Can you think of any incidents that have been reported recently where this may possibly have happened? Invent a story of your own in which a reporter seems to go too far in his/her attempt to get a 'scoop'.

3 *Example* raises some important and uncomfortable questions about why society sometimes feels the need to make an example of someone. Have you ever been made an example of? Improvise a scene which shows someone being made an example of, but make it clear why those who are judging the person think it is the right thing to do.

4 *Example* could be described as a piece of 'documentary theatre', in that it uses a piece of history, and most of the characters in it really lived. The aim is to make an audience think about a real event and feel some of the emotions that the real characters must have felt. Simply hearing about events on the news or reading of them in the paper doesn't always give us a chance to understand the emotions experienced by those involved. Try to think of a real event, recent or past, that you feel deserves exploring in this way.

- In groups make a tableau depicting any scene from the incident
- Take it in turns to leave the tableau and imagine that you are a newspaper photographer. Focus on just one bit of the scene and invent a caption
- Discuss what effect your different photographs might have on an audience (if you have one you could actually use a Polaroid camera for this exercise).

Imagine that just one of the pictures taken is shown in the papers. Improvise the scene in which one or all of the characters involved see it. What happens next?

INDIANS

by Arthur Kopit

CAST (in order of appearance)

SENATOR LOGAN
JOHN GRASS
SENATOR DAWES
SENATOR MORGAN
BUFFALO BILL
* ANNIE OAKLEY
VOICE (OFFSTAGE)
CHIEF JOSEPH
* INDIANS, ROUGHRIDERS AND ROUSTABOUTS

7 speaking parts. Doubling possible.
* non-speaking parts

Most of what people in Europe know about the North American Indian has probably come from films and television shows made in America by white Americans. Through the treatment they are given in the typical Hollywood Western, it is easy to view the Indians as mindless savages who stood in the way of progress represented by brave settlers and pioneers plunging into the wilderness in their wagon trains. The fact that the wilderness is now prosperous ranch land seems to suggest that even though many were killed, the end result was worth it. It seems appropriate that the films that have given us so many ideas about the opening up of America were made in California – the end of the long trail west. When John Wayne made his films he perhaps saw his work as honouring his forefathers who had taken the risks that made the nation great.

But there is another side to the story that is less palatable than the popular one seen in the cinema. Characters like Sitting Bull, Geronimo and Crazy Horse aren't just fictional. They were real men who, in one way or another, fought for what they saw as their birthright – free passage across a vast land. In the space of less than a century the age-old tribes of plains Indians were reduced from populous, thriving nations with their own traditions and histories, to small bands held in barren reservations. Many tribes were wiped out completely by starvation or massacre as they were gradually herded out of their homelands into the areas that the white man didn't want.

Buffalo Bill and Wild Bill Hickok were also real characters. Born William F. Cody, Buffalo Bill acquired his nickname after he slaughtered 4,280 buffaloes to feed the men building the railroad. Unfortunately not only did the men not like the meat, the buffalo reproduces so slowly that the kill seriously damaged the Indians' food supply for years afterwards. In 1883 Cody set up a 'Wild West Show' which used circus techniques and specially written playlets to depict the deeds of the frontiersmen. The great Sioux chief Sitting Bull was allowed to join the show and was, in fact, a friend of the affable Cody. Some old people in this country can remember the visit the Wild West Show made to Britain.

The style of the play

Indians is a complex piece of theatre which uses real people and real events but presents them in a very showy way in order both to create a documentary about the destruction of the North American Indian and to make a critical comment on the trivial way in which history has been treated. Scenes depicting acts from Buffalo Bill's Wild West Show are intercut with scenes showing a meeting between US Government officials and Indians. It bears a similarity to the play *Oh! What a lovely war* which retells the story of the First World War largely through the use of popular song and comic sketches. The aim of both plays is to make the audience see history in a realistic rather than an idealised way. Like *Oh! What a lovely war*, it is visually stunning to watch, and both funny and moving throughout.

The extract

Two scenes are presented here. In the first we see how the US Government can't understand the Indians' claims. The three senators try to keep their patience but basically see the Indians as stupid children. (They even tell the Indians that the President is 'The Great Father'.) However, the Indians' spokesman, John Grass, is anything but stupid and is able to hold his own in the battle of words. In sharp contrast to this intense situation, the second scene presents the audience with the glamour and fun of the Wild

West Show. However, our sympathies are already turning to the Indians and we are moved and chilled by Chief Joseph's speech. The scene ends with an astonishing re-enactment of the Sundance which again contrasts the sham with the authentic.

Scene eight

Lights up again on the Senate Committee.

SENATOR LOGAN   Mister Grass. Let's leave aside the question of the steamboat. You mentioned the treaty at Fort Lyon and said the parts of that treaty had never been fulfilled. Well, I happen to be quite familiar with that particular treaty and happen to know that it is the Indians who did not   5
fulfil its terms, not us.

JOHN GRASS   We did not *want* the cows you sent!

SENATOR LOGAN   You signed the treaty.

JOHN GRASS   We did not understand that we were to give up part of our reservation in exchange for these cows.   10

SENATOR DAWES   Why'd you think we were giving you twenty-five thousand cows?

JOHN GRASS   We were hungry. We thought it was for food.

SENATOR LOGAN   It wasn't explained that *only* if you gave us part of your reservation would you receive these cows?   15

JOHN GRASS   Yes. That was explained.

SENATOR MORGAN   And yet, you thought it was a gift.

JOHN GRASS   Yes.

SENATOR LOGAN   In other words, you thought you could have both the cows and the land?   20

JOHN GRASS   Yes.

SENATOR DAWES   Even though it was explained that you couldn't.

JOHN GRASS   Yes.

SENATOR MORGAN   This is quite hard to follow.   25

SENATOR LOGAN   Mister Grass, tell me, which would you prefer, cows or land?

JOHN GRASS   We prefer them both.

SENATOR LOGAN   Well, what if you can't have them both?

JOHN GRASS   We prefer the land.   30

SENATOR LOGAN   Well then, if you knew you had to give up some land to get these cows, why did you sign the treaty?

JOHN GRASS   The white men made our heads dizzy, and the signing was an accident.

SENATOR LOGAN   An accident?   35

JOHN GRASS   They talked in a threatening way, and whenever we asked questions, shouted and said we were stupid. Suddenly, the Indians around me rushed up and signed the paper. They were like men stumbling in the dark. I could not catch them.   40

SENATOR LOGAN   But you signed it, too.

   Long pause.

SENATOR DAWES   Mister Grass. Tell me. Do the Indians really expect to keep all this land and yet do nothing toward supporting themselves?

JOHN GRASS   We do not have to support ourselves. The Great   45
Father promised to give us everything we ever needed; for that, we gave him the Black Hills.

SENATOR LOGAN   Mister Grass. Which do you prefer – to be self-sufficient or to be given things?

JOHN GRASS   We prefer them both.   50

SENATOR DAWES   Well, you can't *have* both!

BUFFALO BILL   *Please!*

JOHN GRASS   I only know what we were promised.

SENATOR DAWES   That's *not* what you were promised!

JOHN GRASS   We believe it is.   55

BUFFALO BILL   *What's going on here?*

SENATOR MORGAN   Mister Grass. Wouldn't you and your people like to live like the white man?

JOHN GRASS   We are happy like the Indian!

SENATOR LOGAN   He means, you wouldn't like to see your   60
people made *greater*, let's say?

JOHN GRASS   That is not possible! The Cheyenne and the Sioux are as great as people can be, already.

SENATOR MORGAN   Extraordinary, really.

BUFFALO BILL   Mister Grass. Surely . . . *surely* . . . your people   65
would like to *improve their condition!*

JOHN GRASS   We would like what is owed us! If the white men want to give us more, that is fine also.

SENATOR LOGAN   Well, we'll see what we can do.

SENATOR MORGAN   Let's call the next. This is getting us nowhere. 70

JOHN GRASS   We would especially like the money the Great Father says he is holding for us!

SENATOR DAWES   I'm afraid that may be difficult, since, in the past, we've found that when an Indian's been given money, 75 he's spent it all on liquor.

JOHN GRASS   When he's been given money, it's been so little there's been little else he could buy.

SENATOR MORGAN   Whatever, the Great Father does not like his Indian children getting drunk! 80

JOHN GRASS   Then tell the Great Father, who says he wishes us to live like white men, that when an Indian gets drunk, he is merely imitating the white men he's observed!

Laughter from the INDIANS. LOGAN *raps his gavel.*

SENATOR DAWES   STOP IT!

No effect. LOGAN *raps more.*

What in God's name do they think we're doing here? STOP 85 IT!

Over the INDIANS' *noise, the noise of a Wild West Show is heard; lights fade to black.*

Scene nine

Wild West Show music and crisscrossing multicoloured spotlights. The rodeo ring rises from the stage, its lights glittering. Wild West Show banners descend above the ring.

VOICE   And now, ladies and gentlemen, let's hear it for Buffalo Bill's fantastic company of authentic western heroes . . . the fabulous ROUGHRIDERS OF THE WORLD!

Enter, on heroically artificial horses, the ROUGHRIDERS — *themselves heroically oversized.*

*They gallop about the ring in majestic, intricate forma-
tion, whoopin' and shooting' as they do.*

With the ever-lovely . . . ANNIE OAKLEY!

ANNIE OAKLEY *performs some startling trick shots as the
others ride in circles about her.*

And now, once again, here he is – the star of our show, the   90
Ol' Scout himself; I mean the indestructible and ever-
popular —

Drum roll

— BUFFALO BILL!

Enter, on horseback, BUFFALO BILL. *He is in his Wild West
finery.*
He tours the ring in triumph while his ROUGHRIDERS *ride
after him, finally exiting to leave him in the centre, alone.*

BUFFALO BILL   THANK YOU, THANK YOU! A GREAT show
lined up tonight! With all-time favourite Johnny Baker,   95
Texas Jack and his twelve-string guitar, the Dancin'
Cavanaughs, Sheriff Brad and the Deadwood Mail Coach,
Harry Philamee's Trained Prairie Dogs, the Abilene County
Girls' School Trick Roping and Lasso Society, Pecos Pete
and the —   100
VOICE   *Bill.*
BUFFALO BILL [*startled*]   Hm?
VOICE   Bring on the Indians.
BUFFALO BILL   What?
VOICE   The *Indians.*   105
BUFFALO BILL   Ah.

BUFFALO BILL *looks uneasily toward the wings as his
company of* INDIANS *enters solemnly and in ceremonial
warpaint; they carry the Sun Dance pole. At its summit is
a buffalo skull.*

And now, while my fabulous company of authentic . . .
American Indians go through the ceremonial preparations of
the Sun Dance, which they will re-enact in all its death-

defying goriness – let's give a warm welcome back to a   110
courageous warrior, the magnificent Chief Joseph —

Some COWBOY ROUSTABOUTS *set up an inverted tub; music
for* CHIEF JOSEPH's *entrance.*

— who will recite his ... celebrated speech. CHIEF
JOSEPH!

Enter CHIEF JOSEPH, *old and hardly able to walk.*

CHIEF JOSEPH   In the moon of the cherries blossoming, in the
year of our surrender, I, Chief Joseph, and what remained of   115
my people, the Nez Percés, were sent to a prison in
Oklahoma, though General Howard had promised we could
return to Idaho, where we'd always lived. In the moon of
the leaves falling, still in the year of our surrender, William
Cody came to see me. He was a nice man. With eyes that   120
seemed ... frightened, I ... don't know why. He told me I
was courageous and said he admired me. Then he explained
all about his Wild West Show, in which the great Sitting Bull
appeared, and said if I agreed to join, he would have me
released from prison, and see that my people received food. I   125
asked what I could do, as I was not a very good rider or
marksman. And he looked away and said 'Just repeat, twice
a day, three times on Sundays, what you said that afternoon
when our army caught you at the Canadian border, where
you'd been heading, and where you and your people would   130
have all been safe.' So I agreed. For the benefit of my
people. ... And for the next year, twice a day, three times
on Sundays, said this to those sitting around me in the dark,
where I could not see them, a light shining so brightly in my
eyes!   135

Pause.
He climbs up on the tub.
Accompanied by exaggerated and inappropriate gestures.

'Tell General Howard I know his heart. I am tired of
fighting. Our chiefs have been killed. Looking Glass is dead.
The old men are all dead. It is cold and we have no blankets.
The children are freezing. My people, some of them, have

fled to the hills and have no food or warm clothing. No one 140
knows where they are – perhaps frozen. I want to have time
to look for my children and see how many of them I can
find. Maybe I shall find them among the dead. Hear me, my
chiefs. I am tired. My heart is sick and sad. From where the
sun now stands, I will fight no more forever. . . .' 145

He climbs down from the tub.

After which, the audience always applauded me.

Exit CHIEF JOSEPH. *Pause.*

BUFFALO BILL The Sun Dance . . . was the one religious
ceremony common to all the tribes of the plains. The Sioux,
the Crow, the Blackfeet, the Kiowa, the Blood, the Cree, the
Chippewa, the Arapaho, the Pawnee, the Cheyenne. It was 150
their way of proving they were . . . Indians.

Pause.

The bravest would take the ends of long leather thongs and
hook them through their chest muscles, then, pull till they'd
ripped them out. The greater the pain they could endure, the
greater they felt the Spirits would favour them. Give them 155
what they needed. . . . Grant them . . . salvation.

Pause.

Since the Government has officially outlawed this ritual, we
will merely imitate it.

Pause.

And no one . . . will be hurt.

He steps back.
The dance begins. The INDIANS *take the barbed ends of
long leather thongs that dangle from the top of the Sun
Dance pole and hook them through plainly visible chest
harnesses. Then they pull back against the centre and
dance about it, flailing their arms and moaning as if in
great pain.*
Suddenly JOHN GRASS *enters.* A ROUSTABOUT *tries to stop
him.*

The INDIANS *are astonished to see this intruder;* BUFFALO BILL *stunned.*

JOHN GRASS *pulls the* INDIANS *out of their harness, rips open his shirt, and sticks the barbs through his chest muscles. He chants and dances. The other* INDIANS, *realizing what he's doing, blow on reed whistles, urge him on. Finally he collapses, blood pouring from his chest.*

The INDIANS *gather around him in awe.*

BUFFALO BILL *walks slowly toward* JOHN GRASS; *stares down at him.*

The INDIANS *remove the Sun Dance pole and trappings.*

BUFFALO BILL *crouches and cradles* JOHN GRASS *in his arms. As lights fade to black.*

Understanding the text

1 The Indians and the Senators have very different perceptions of their situation. Pick out two things that John Grass says that show how they really don't understand each other's way of thinking.

2 Look at Buffalo Bill's lines in Scene Eight. In what ways does his attitude to the Indians seem to differ from the Senators'?

3 The Voice seems to have two separate functions in Scene Nine. First it introduces the Wild West Show as a sort of Master of Ceremonies. What do you think its other function is?

4 Chief Joseph's line, 'After which, the audience always applauded me' seems to have the power to move audiences. Look at both parts of the speech again carefully and discuss why this line is so effective. Compare Chief Joseph's life in the circus with how he reports the life of the tribe to General Howard.

5 Look at the way tension is created at the end of both scenes. What is the effect of the abrupt switch from the meeting to the show?

Producing the scene

1 One way of achieving quick scene changes, as in this extract, is to have a split-level stage. Draw a diagram of how you could use a two-level stage to give the audience a good view of both scenes. How much room will you need for each scene?

2 Design or describe two contrasting costumes needed for these scenes. Consider how you might go about researching such costumes if you were asked actually to produce them as authentically as possible.

3 Look at the stage direction, *Enter, on heroically artificial horses, the* ROUGHRIDERS — *themselves heroically oversized.* Design either a suitably heroic hobby-horse or explain in words or with diagrams how the Roughriders might be made to appear 'oversized'.

4 How could lighting effects be used to contrast the two scenes? Describe what colours and types of lights you might use and, if possible, design a specimen lighting plot and cue sheet for these scenes.

5 As a director, what advice would you give to the actor playing Chief Joseph? What *exaggerated and inappropriate gestures* could be used and where? Work in pairs, one taking the role of the director and the other the actor attempting to put these ideas into practice.

6 In small groups imagine the Senators, and perhaps some cavalry soldiers, are posing to have their photograph taken before meeting the Indians. Decide, by acting this out, how they would position themselves for such a photograph. Adapt their postures in order to achieve an appropriate tableau for when the lights come up on Scene Eight. Discuss what the tableau says about the characters depicted.

7 The final scene in which John Grass performs the sundance has, no doubt, kept many directors awake at night because it is so difficult technically. You may have seen the film *A Man Called Horse* in which the ritual is acted out. Look carefully at the stage directions and discuss ways of achieving the effect described in them.

Further development

1 A major theme of the play is the problem of two viewpoints clashing head on. Make a list of as many other situations as you can think of where this happens. Divide the list into three sections:
  • those which are purely personal, for example a disagreement with your parents over something.
  • those which are social or cultural, for instance which day of the week should be set aside for worship?
  • those which seem to be both personal and social, for example a conscientious objector refusing to fight for his/her country.

2 John Grass is driven to performing the sundance in a desperate attempt to draw attention to his people's situation. Look at the list you made in

Question 1. Are there any situations there that you know, or can imagine, have led to such desperate acts? In pairs choose one situation and improvise a scene in which actor A is explaining to actor B how and why they intend to make a point. Actor B should be sympathetic but nevertheless try to find reasons why such an act would be the wrong thing to do.

3 Replay the scene above, swopping roles, but making actor B totally unsympathetic to the cause. Compare the two scenes in terms of dramatic potential. What effect would each option have on an audience?

4 Switching styles quickly in order to 'shock' an audience into thinking about the content of a play is an effective technique. In this extract the depressing reality of the negotiations is sharply contrasted with the flashy and trivial presentation of the Wild West Show. Select a situation from the list prepared in Question 1 and write or improvise two scenes which treat the conflict in contrasting ways. For example, you could compare a news documentary report about an incident with a situation comedy which makes fun of the situation, or even compare the actual events of an incident with how they might be reported on the news.

5 With the aid of the teacher, divide the class into two. Imagine that one half is a group of pioneers who have taken considerable risks and made many sacrifices in order to 'open up the West' and make a living there. The other half is an Indian group which has lived on the land for centuries and has never felt the need to change its way of life. Each group has been given the opportunity of making a TV documentary about:

- what the current problem is
- how the problem came about
- what they think might happen next.

Show the documentaries to the other group. What is their reaction:

- in their character as an Indian or a Pioneer?
- as a member of the class?

6 *Indians* is a play which arose from the author's despair and frustration at real events as he saw them. A great deal of the power of the play comes from the fact that the events and characters are real, even if the way they are presented uses theatrical techniques. You could undertake an extended project of your own in which you research more thoroughly into one of the situations noted in Question 1 and find a way of presenting 'fact' in a theatrical way. Where would you start your research? Who could you talk to? What actual incidents could be dramatised? What theatrical techniques could you apply to moments in real life in order to make your point about them more clear to an audience?

A DREAM PLAY

by August Strindberg

The curious thing about dreams is that whilst the mind is rapidly flitting from one bizarre incident to another, the whole thing seems to have a sort of logic to it. Most people now accept that the contents of dreams are a kind of montage of other experiences – either things that have actually happened to the dreamer or things that the dreamer has been thinking about. Just as a whole new picture can be made up of other bits, so a whole new experience can be created in a dream world by reassembling bits from the real world. Sometimes in the middle of a dream you also seem to know that it's a dream you're having – it's like being engrossed in a film or play but at the same time knowing that you are watching actors and not real people.

The actual study of how the mind appears to function is quite a young science. An early psychologist who has had a great influence on modern thinking was Sigmund Freud. He was particularly interested in dreams and how they relate to reality. His work made people see a difference between the conscious part of our minds (the bit we are aware of) and the subconscious (the bit that makes us do things without our realising why we do them).

42

Just as Freud was changing the way scientists and doctors thought about human behaviour, so several artists and writers were using their art to delve deeper into what being a human really involved. In drama this tended to mean a reaction against writing plays involving the straight-forward unfolding of a story, and a move towards experimenting with more striking images and issues.

One of the most inspiring writers of this new wave was the Swedish playwright, August Strindberg. Many of Strindberg's plays show characters being driven by a particular psychological force such as jealousy or spite; what makes them do things is of more interest to the audience than what they actually do.

The style of the play

A Dream Play was written in 1901 whilst Strindberg was going through an extremely stormy time with his wife (he had a number of tempestuous relationships with women). Not for the first time, he was swinging from ecstatic happiness to deep depression. In his own introduction to the play he says: 'In this dream play, the author has . . . attempted to imitate the inconsequent yet transparently logical shape of a dream. Everything can happen, everything is possible and probable. Time and place do not exist. . .'. When it was first published it was generally regarded as completely unstageable, largely because of the way it cuts from one exotic location to another so quickly. However, modern audiences are rather different in their attitudes in at least two important respects. First, we are used to watching films which make similar jumps through time and space. Second, a number of playwrights after Strindberg went on to develop the idea that we can hold both the real and the unreal world in our minds at the same time; we can be absorbed in a play yet know that we are watching actors.

The key to understanding and staging *A Dream Play* is surely to remember that in a dream anything can happen. The actors' and director's job may be more to do with sparking the audience's imagination than telling a story.

The extract

One of the key figures in the play is the Daughter. As a 'child of God' she has come to visit Earth and to try to understand life here. In this extract she is taken to an island called Fairhaven. As its name suggests it seems to be an idyllic place. According to Strindberg's stage direction a second, contrasting island, Foulstrand, can be seen in the distance. However, Fairhaven's charms seem subjective – that is to say that its appeal depends on your personality and situation. Pursuing this theme, Strindberg moves the scene on to a stereotypical holiday paradise, but peoples the scene with unexpected characters to show that what is heaven for one may be hell for another.

OFFICER Look at this man! He is the most envied of all who live here. [*The* BLIND MAN *is led in.*] He owns these hundred Italian villas; he owns all these bays, inlets, beaches, forests, the fish in the water, the birds in the air and the game in the woods. These thousand people are his tenants and the sun   5
rises over his seas and sinks over his lands –
DAUGHTER Does he complain too?
OFFICER Yes, and with reason, for he cannot see.
QUARANTINE MASTER He is blind.
DAUGHTER The most envied of all!   10
OFFICER Now he wants to see the ship sail out, with his son on board.
BLIND MAN I do not see, but I hear. I hear how the anchor claws the sea-bed as when one draws the hook from a fish and the heart follows up through the throat. My son, my   15
only child, is going abroad across the wide sea. I can accompany him only in my thoughts. Now I hear the cable screech, and – something flutters and swishes like clothes drying on a line – wet handkerchieves, perhaps – and I hear how it snuffles and sobs, like people crying – perhaps the   20
small waves lapping against the nets, or is it the girls on the shore, the abandoned, the comfortless? Once I asked a child why the sea was salt, and the child who had a father at sea replied at once: 'The sea is salt because sailors cry so much.' 'Why do sailors cry so much?' 'Oh,' said the child, 'because   25
they are always having to go away. That's why they always dry their handkerchieves up on the masts.' 'Why do people cry when they are sad?' I asked him. 'Oh,' said the child, 'because their eyes have to be washed sometimes so that they can see more clearly.'   30

The ship has set sail and glides away. The GIRLS *on the shore wave their handkerchieves and dab away their tears. On the foremast the signal 'Yes' is raised, a red ball on a white background.* ALICE *waves joyfully in reply.*

DAUGHTER [*to* OFFICER]   What does that flag mean?

OFFICER   It means yes. That is the lieutenant's 'Yes' in red, like the red heart's blood drawn on the blue cloth of heaven.

DAUGHTER   How does 'No' look, then?

OFFICER   It is blue, like the spoiled blood in his veins. But see   35
how happy Alice is!

DAUGHTER   And how Edith is crying.

THE BLIND MAN   Meeting and parting. Parting and meeting. That is life. I met his mother. And then she went away. I kept our son. Now he is going.   40

DAUGHTER   He will surely come back.

BLIND MAN   Who is that? I have heard that voice before, in my dreams, in my youth, when the summer holidays began, in the first year of marriage when my child was born. Every time she smiled, I heard the voice.   45

The ADVOCATE *enters, goes over to the* BLIND MAN *and whispers.*

BLIND MAN   I see.

ADVOCATE   Yes that's what they've done. [*Goes over to* DAUGHTER] Now you have seen almost everything, but you haven't experienced the worst thing.

DAUGHTER   What can that be?   50

ADVOCATE   Repetition. Repeating the pattern. Go back! Learn your lesson again. Come.

DAUGHTER   Where?

ADVOCATE   To your duties.

DAUGHTER   What is duty?   55

ADVOCATE   It is everything you shrink from. Everything you don't want to do and must. It is to abstain, to renounce, to go without, to leave behind. Everything unpleasant, repulsive, tedious –

DAUGHTER   Are there no pleasant duties?   60

ADVOCATE   They become pleasant when you have performed them –

45

DAUGHTER   When they no longer exist. So duty is always unpleasant. What is pleasant?

ADVOCATE   Sin is pleasant.   65

DAUGHTER   Sin?

ADVOCATE   Which must be punished, yes. If I have had a pleasant day and evening, I suffer the pangs of hell and a sick conscience the next day.

DAUGHTER   How strange!   70

ADVOCATE   Yes, I wake up in the morning with a headache; and then the repetition begins, but a perverse repetition. In such a way that everything that the previous evening was beautiful, pleasant, witty, appears this morning in my memory as ugly, repulsive, stupid. The pleasure rots, and the   75 joy crumbles. What people call success is always the prelude to one's next setback. My successes became my defeat. People have an instinctive fear of other men's successes; they think it unjust that fate should favour one man, so they try to restore the balance by setting rocks in their path. To have   80 talent is dangerous. One can easily starve to death. However, go back to your duties, or I shall sue you, and we shall go through all the three courts, one, two, three.

DAUGHTER   Go back? To the iron stove with the pot of cabbage, the child's nappies – ?   85

ADVOCATE   Yes. Today is washing day. We must wash all the handkerchieves –

DAUGHTER   Oh, must I do all that again?

ADVOCATE   Life consists of doing things again. Look at the schoolmaster in there. Yesterday he got his Doctorate, was   90 crowned with laurel to the sound of cannon, ascended Parnassus and was embraced by the King. And today he starts school again, asks what is two times two, and so he must continue until he dies.

DAUGHTER   It is not easy to be a human being.   95

ALL   True!

DAUGHTER   I shall not return to that dirt and degradation with you. I want to return whence I came, but – first I must open the door that I may know the secret. I want the door to be opened!   100

ADVOCATE   Then you must retrace your steps, return by the same path, and endure all the horrors of trial, the repetitions, the repetitions, the repetitions –
DAUGHTER   So be it. But first I must go alone into the desert to rediscover myself. We shall meet again. [*To the* POET.] Come   105
with me.

From the rear of the stage are heard distant cries of anguish.

DAUGHTER   What was that?
ADVOCATE   The unhappy people of Foulstrand.
DAUGHTER   Why do they cry so much more piteously today?
ADVOCATE   Because the sun is shining here, because here there   110
is music, dancing and youth. It enhances their suffering.
DAUGHTER   We must free them.
ADVOCATE   Try. Someone tried once, and they hanged Him on
a cross.
DAUGHTER   Who did?
ADVOCATE   All right-thinking people.   115
DAUGHTER   Who are they?
ADVOCATE   Don't you know all right-thinking people? Well,
you must meet some.
DAUGHTER   Was it they who refused you your laurel wreath?
ADVOCATE   Yes.   120
DAUGHTER   Then I do know them.

A shore by the Mediterranean. Downstage left is a white wall, with orange trees in fruit visible over the top of it. Upstage, villas and a terraced casino. Right, a big pile of coal with two wheelbarrows. Upstage right, a glimpse of the blue sea.

Two COAL-CARRIERS, *stripped to the waist, their faces, hands and the naked parts of their bodies all black, sit on their wheelbarrows in despair. The* DAUGHTER *and* ADVOCATE *watch them from upstage.*

DAUGHTER   This is Paradise!
FIRST COAL-CARRIER   This is hell!
SECOND COAL-CARRIER   Ninety in the shade.

FIRST COAL-CARRIER Shall we have a swim?   125

SECOND COAL-CARRIER They'd arrest us. We're not allowed to bathe here.

FIRST COAL-CARRIER Couldn't we pick some of those oranges?

SECOND COAL-CARRIER They'd arrest us.

FIRST COAL-CARRIER I can't work in this heat. I'm giving it up.   130

SECOND COAL-CARRIER Then they'll arrest you. [*Pause.*] And you'll have no food.

FIRST COAL-CARRIER No food? We who work most must eat least; and the rich who do nothing, they get most.

DAUGHTER Tell me. What have you done that you are so   135 black and your lot so hard?

FIRST COAL-CARRIER What have we done? We were born of poor and not very good parents. Maybe got punished once or twice.

DAUGHTER Punished?   140

FIRST COAL-CARRIER Yes. The unpunished sit up there in the casino and eat eight courses with wine.

DAUGHTER [*to* ADVOCATE] Can this be true?

ADVOCATE Broadly speaking, yes.

DAUGHTER You mean that every human being has at some   145 time done something deserving of imprisonment?

ADVOCATE Yes.

DAUGHTER You too?

ADVOCATE Yes.

DAUGHTER Is it true that these poor men are not allowed to   150 bathe here?

ADVOCATE Not even with their clothes on. Only those who have tried to drown themselves escape a fine. And they get a thrashing in the police station.

DAUGHTER Couldn't they go outside the town and bathe   155 somewhere in the countryside?

ADVOCATE There isn't any countryside, it's all enclosed.

DAUGHTER I mean in the common land.

ADVOCATE There isn't any common land. It's all privately owned.   160

DAUGHTER Even the sea?

ADVOCATE Everything. You can't take a boat out or step ashore without paying for it. Pretty, eh?

DAUGHTER   This is not Paradise.

ADVOCATE   I assure you it isn't.   165

DAUGHTER   But why do people do nothing to improve their lot?

ADVOCATE   Oh, some do. But all the improvers end in prison or the madhouse.

DAUGHTER   Who puts them in prison?   170

ADVOCATE   All right-thinking men, all honourable –

DAUGHTER   Who puts them in the madhouse?

ADVOCATE   Their own despair at the hopelessness of endeavour.

DAUGHTER   Does no one suspect that there may be some secret   175
reason why things must be as they are?

ADVOCATE   Yes, the ones who are well off always think that.

DAUGHTER   That life is good as it is – ?

FIRST COAL-CARRIER   And yet we are society's corner-stone. If
you didn't get any coal carried, the stove would go out in   180
the kitchen, the fire in the living-room, the machine would
stop in the factory; then the lights would go out in the
streets, in the shops, in the home; darkness and cold would
descend on you. And so we sweat in hell. What do *you* give
us?   185

ADVOCATE [*to* DAUGHTER]   Help them. [*Pause.*] I know everyone can't be totally equal, but need they be so unequal?

A GENTLEMAN *and his* WIFE *pass across the stage.*

WIFE   Do you feel like playing cards?

GENTLEMAN   No, I must take a walk to be able to eat lunch.

FIRST COAL-CARRIER   To be *able* to eat lunch?   190

SECOND COAL-CARRIER   To be *able* – ?

CHIILDREN *enter and scream at the sight of the blackened
workers.*

FIRST COAL-CARRIER   They scream at the sight of us. They
scream.

SECOND COAL-CARRIER   God damn it! It's time to bring out the
knives and operate on this rotten body.   195

FIRST COAL-CARRIER   God damn them! [*Spits.*]

ADVOCATE [*to* DAUGHTER]   Mad, isn't it? People aren't so bad.
   Its just –
DAUGHTER   Just..
ADVOCATE   The way things are run.   200
DAUGHTER [*hides her face as she goes*]   This is not Paradise.
COAL-CARRIERS   No. It is hell.

Understanding the text

1 Pick out three examples from the script in which Strindberg suggests that there can't be a good side to life without there also being a bad. For example, the Officer says, 'see how happy Alice is', to which the Daughter replies, 'And how Edith is crying.'
2 What evidence is there in the script that the Daughter has never visited Earth before?
3 Strindberg introduces the characters as types rather than as named people. Pick out three things which suggest that these people are stereotypes rather than real. What does this suggest about the aim of the play?
4 Just as the Daughter seems to know nothing about life, so the Advocate seems to understand it very well. What basic lessons does the Daughter learn in this extract?
5 Who do you think the Advocate is talking about when he refers to 'right-thinking people'? What would you say Strindberg's own opinion of 'right-thinking people' is?

Producing the scene

1 How could you use costumes to suggest:
   • the type of characters who appear in the extract?
   • the fact that they are part of a dream?
2 Go through the extract and note any places (other than those indicated in the text) where you think a sound effect could be used. For instance, you might decide that cries of farewell are suitable as the ship sets sail. Experiment with ways of making appropriate effects just by using your voice or body in some way. Sometimes a chorus of human sound effects can be theatrically very interesting and add an element of strangeness to a scene.

3 Suggest, and possibly try out, a lighting plan for this scene. In order to capture the dreamlike quality you could experiment not only with strange colours but also with unusual angles. For example, try shining a light directly down on the Daughter's head, or lighting the Blind Man from behind. How does this enhance their image, if at all?

4 In what ways do the Coal-Carriers contrast with the Gentleman and his Wife? In groups of four make a tableau of the characters as if the action was frozen on the line 'I must take a walk to be able to eat lunch'. Refine each actor's position, expression and their relationship to the other characters in order to illustrate the contrast most strikingly.

5 Throughout the extract the Daughter seems to be in the middle of some fantastic journey. Either in groups of about six, or as a whole class, invent a way of suggesting such a journey through the Daughter's actual movement.

6 When the play was first written many people said it was unstageable. Can you find two examples from the extract that support such a view? What technical changes since Strindberg's time would make the play easier to present?

Further development

1 With the help of the class teacher, form a large circle. One person volunteers to start an action in the middle – cleaning a window, or rowing a boat, for example. After 30 seconds or so the teacher or group leader calls 'FREEZE', and points to another person in the circle whilst the person in the middle freezes. Person B enters the arena and restarts the action in a new scene; so, for example, the person who froze whilst cleaning a window may be reactivated as if she was grabbing an apple from a tree. The action continues until the leader calls 'FREEZE' again and a third person enters. Go on until the whole group is involved. You may have improvised in this way before, but in this case try to pick up on the idea that in a dream people and places can change suddenly, but in a way that appears perfectly normal.

2 In groups of four or five, one person starts to tell a story which starts 'I had the strangest dream last night . . .'. As she continues, saying the first things that come into her head, the other members of the group try to put actions to the description. If you genuinely say the first things that come into your head you may find you stumble upon some fascinating ideas and images. You may well uncover some ideas here that would be worth developing into a rehearsed improvisation.

3 In pairs, improvise a scene in which Strindberg is talking to a psychiatrist about his dreams. (The dreams can be as crazy as you like; you may find they provide the basis for further improvisation.)

4 In small groups prepare, through improvisation, a scene entitled 'One Man's Meat is Another Man's Poison'.

5 What would be your idea of the perfect Heaven or perfect Hell? Is Heaven full of clouds and harps and Hell all fires and screams? Perhaps your personal Hell would be to be trapped in the place you hate the most doing the things you hate the most. In small groups try to create a human sculpture of either Heaven or Hell. Use your voices to make an appropriate 'soundtrack' that matches the still image.

6 Find a piece of dream-like music and devise a piece of movement which might suggest a fantastic journey, such as the Daughter's, to go with it.

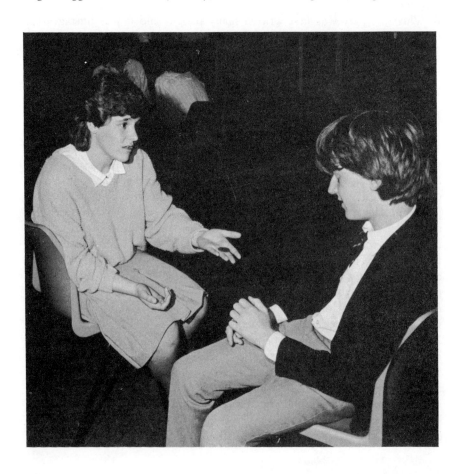

SHE'S DEAD

by Paul Abelman

CAST (in order of appearance)

1

2

2 speaking parts. No doubling.

She's Dead is one of the short plays published in a book called *Tests*. It was first published in 1966 and reflects the way people involved with the theatre at that time were putting a great deal of energy into exploring new forms and ideas.

Until the middle of the 1950s British theatre-going audiences were used to seeing plays which followed very conventional patterns. They were usually set in middle-class homes and were about middle-class people's problems. Sometimes they are referred to as 'well-made plays' which suggests that they were constructed in a careful but rather predictable way. However, a number of new ideas began to influence the British theatre. John Osborne's play *Look Back in Anger* is often seen as a play that shifted attention away from the middle classes and opened the way for the exploration of broader issues and viewpoints. In the East End of London, a director called Joan Littlewood was successfully staging the work of new, young writers, and the strange, 'absurd' theatre of Samuel Beckett was starting to appear in theatre clubs. The Royal Shakespeare Company had a young and revolutionary director called Peter Brook who, in the early 1960s, presented a season of plays under the title of 'The Theatre of Cruelty'. It must have been very exciting to see the theatre changing from being a place which provided entertainment for a select group of people into a place where new ideas could be developed and the assumptions and attitudes of the audience challenged.

The style of the play

She's Dead seems to extract humour from a very serious incident. Modern audiences or readers might see in it something of the style of *Monty Python's Flying Circus*. This isn't surprising because the Python team were influenced by many of the things that were happening in the theatre at this time. However, the play is perhaps more than just a piece of daft humour – the last line, in particular, suggests that the author had deeper themes in mind when he wrote it.

Because it is a 'test', it is impossible to say how the play should be acted out or what the characters should be like. It is a piece of unfinished theatre which demands that the actors and director decide what they want to do with it and add their own creative and imaginative abilities to the performance.

---

1 By jove, you've murdered that woman!
2 It's dreadful!
1 Why did you do it?
2 She provoked me. This is terrible.
1 You've killed her. You've taken a human life!   5
2 It's appalling! This is the most frightful thing that ever happened to me.
1 What have you done, man?
2 I think I've killed this woman.
1 Jove, how ghastly!   10
2 This is horrible. Yesterday – a year ago – how could I have dreamt . . .
1 Look here, what have you done?
2 My God, she's dead!
1 How awful!   15
2 This is terrible.
1 Well, there's one fortunate thing.
2 Is there some consolation?
1 There's one very happy aspect.
2 Do you detect some glint of hope?   20
1 I'm a policeman. I can arrest you and make sure you pay the full penalty for your crime.
2 I say, that is lucky.

1 Strange that I should happen past, just after you'd done this
  dreadful thing. 25
2 It's almost miraculous, isn't it? Things are never quite as
  bad as they seem at first glance.
1 I'll see that you suffer.
2 I feel I can depend on you.
1 You'll sweat torments in a reeking prison, I'll ensure that. 30
2 It's very good of you.
1 By jove, what's happened here?
2 I've killed this woman.
1 What have you done?
2 I've taken a human life. I've broken the sternest law of God 35
  and man.
1 Thank God, I'm a policeman.
2 Thank God for that!
1 Anguish is your portion from now on, until we take *your*
  life in some disgusting way. 40
2 How will you do it?
1 We'll probably strangle you with a length of rope.
  Nightmares are mere diversion compared to what's waiting
  for you.
2 It's lucky you passed by. 45
1 My God, man, what have you done?
2 Constable, I – I've murdered this woman.
1 Why did you do it?
2 She picked a flower.
1 Provocation is no excuse. 50
2 She was my mother.
1 You've killed your mother. Matricide, you'll squirm! Your
  brain will buzz with horror until you crave the noose as a
  benefaction.
2 I loved this girl. She was a typist. 55
1 You've destroyed a typist, a useful citizen. Think of the
  letters that will blossom no more beneath her nimble
  fingers.
2 This woman was a barmaid.
1 The handle of the beer-pump will ne'er more feel her touch. 60
2 What have I done?
1 You've taken a human life. Now, the facts: How did you
  kill her?

2 With my penknife! Officer, officer, it was unpremeditated. I
merely took out my knife to admire the silver blade and   65
then I felt I should try it out. So I stabbed Lilly twenty-four
times.

1 Look at her blood, her innocent blood!

2 I stabbed her twenty-four times.

1 See, her blood's come out. That'll teach you to play with   70
penknives.

2 Her blood – I didn't think it would all come out.

1 She was a blithe girl, a healthy thing – tell me what she
was?

2 A song!   75

1 Yes, she was a song, a healthy thing. What was this girl?

2 Light.

1 Of course, she was light – she was the air, the breeze, the
ripple in the air, but there was blood inside her.

2 I pierced her veins.   80

1 What have you done?

2 Officer, I have a confession to make.

1 Oh yes, sir?

2 Yes, you see I seem to have – inadvertently of course – slain
this girl.   85

1 I see, sir. You realize, sir, that I shall have to report this?

2 Is that absolutely necessary, officer?

1 It's the regulations, sir. I know that we often seem
unnecessarily meticulous to the public but we have to
register all misdemeanours.   90

2 I say, I hope this doesn't mean I shall have to appear in
court?

1 Oh no, sir, I shouldn't think anything like that. We get
dozens of these little incidents.

2 She was called Lilly, I think. You may want that for your   95
records.

1 Why did you kill her, sir? I might as well take all the facts.

2 Why. Oh, I don't know. How can one assess every fleeting
impulse? I met her in a pub, brought her out here to this
remote spot, assaulted her –   100

1 Carnally?

2 Yes, you know, rape and then I thought I might as well kill
her as anything else.

1   Right you are, sir, I've got that. Perhaps you'd give me your
    name and address, sir? Just for our files?   105

2   Is that really necessary?

1   Well I would be grateful, sir. My sergeant's a stickler for
    detail.

2   Very well, my name is Bill.

1   Bill, sir?   110

2   Bombay Bill, also known as The Slaughterer.

1   And your address, sir?

2   Skull Lane.

1   I say, what have you done?

2   Has something been done?   115

1   There's a dead girl here.

2   Did I do that?

1   Have you killed this human being?

2   Have I deprived someone of life?

1   At your feet, man, a dead girl!   120

2   A girl you say? One wanting life?

1   Why did you do it?

2   You imply that there's some way of knowing why things
    are done?

1   There's a gun here.   125

2   I fancy it's a revolver.

1   Is this your gun?

2   I have seen that weapon before.

1   Was this the cause of death?

2   A bullet leapt from its mouth.   130

1   This finger, this index finger on your hand – did it squeeze
    the weapon's trigger?

2   Pressure, generated by the muscles of my body, authorized
    by the synapses of my singing nerves, moved that little
    lever. The gun spat metal, a gob of metal which parted her 135
    soft tissues. I think it was then she died.

1   Have you slain this woman?

2   I? I have slain no-one. It was the gunmaker.

1   You killed this girl!

2   It was not I. It was a Hebrew who made the law she broke. 140

1   Then I must arrest you.

2 And are you really authorized to put a stop to history?
1 Jove, what have you done?
2 What I was told to do by the roots groping in the earth.
1 You've killed this girl. 145
2 By the numb stones nesting on the plain.
1 You'll pay for this.
2 By my accomplice the rain and his wild pal the wind.
1 To the cells!
2 Yes, come, brother, to the cells but first – wipe the blood 150 from your hands too.

Understanding the text

1 There are several instances when comedy is achieved by someone making a remark that doesn't seem to match the seriousness of the situation, for example, 'See, her blood's come out, that'll teach you to play with penknives.' Find at least three other lines that create humour in this way.

2 The play suggests that you can view the same incident in totally different ways depending on who and where you are. List the different reactions to the murder shown in the play.

3 The play is full of contradictions. For example, the girl is described as the murderer's mother, a typist and a barmaid. Things just don't appear to make sense! Look through the play again and note the contradictions about who the girl is and how she died. What do you think is being suggested by giving her so many identities?

4 The language of *She's Dead* has a strange and sometimes poetic quality to it. Things are described in unexpected ways; for example, the girl is described as being 'a song'. Pick out at least three lines which strike you as being 'poetic' or unusual in their use of language.

5 Look carefully at the last line. The murderer calls the 'policeman' his 'brother' and then tells him to wipe the blood from his own hands. Do you think these characters really are a murderer and a policeman or might they be representing somebody or something else? Are there any other lines in the play that suggest we are all somehow responsible for what happens to people?

Producing the scene

1 Given that the author makes no suggestions for the set of costumes, where would you set the play and how would you costume 1 and 2? Your suggestions here should depend on your conclusions in the last question.

2 Discuss various ways of staging the play; for example, as a piece of theatre in the round; as a 'promenade performance' that might take place in the theatre foyer or even somewhere where people don't expect to see theatre at all; or on a conventional stage. What would be the advantages and disadvantages of these various ways of staging the play?

3 How important do you think it is actually to have a body on the stage? What would be the advantages and disadvantages of actually having it there?

4 Go through the script again and make a mark every time you think the characters are changing their attitude. If the whole play was acted with 1 and 2 keeping the same character throughout, it might be rather tedious to listen to and watch. Choose one of the changes you have identified and rehearse the few lines before and the few after, freezing at the precise moment when the change takes place. As you 'reactivate' from the freeze, adopt a completely different tone and type of voice and change your position and way of moving accordingly.

5 Using the same short section of the play, experiment with playing it at different speeds. Try delivering it in a fast, obviously comical way and compare this with a slow, heavy and menacing delivery. Are there places in the play where a change of pace might be effective?

6 Developing from Question 4, suggest a number of different character stereotypes that 1 and 2 could adopt in different places. (It might be worth looking at *The Body*, which also explores this technique.) For example, 2 could be a smooth businessman type when he says 'Is that absolutely necessary, officer'. Choose another short extract and rehearse it in pairs using these stereotypes. What effects can you achieve by using an obvious or unexpected characterisation in lines like 'My name is Bill . . . Bombay Bill, also known as The Slaughterer'.

7 Look again at lines 97 to 103. What is your immediate reaction to these lines? Is the author just making a sick joke or is he trying to achieve something else (if so, what)? Experiment with different ways of playing these lines; for example, in a violent and maniacal way or in a calm and official way. You may find it interesting to compare the way girls and boys tackle these same few lines.

8 Experiment with the delivery of the last line, 'wipe the blood from your hands too'. Can you find a way of delivering this line so that the audience are also made to feel they have blood on their hands and are equally responsible for the girl's death?

Further development

1 In pairs improvise a scene in which A accuses B of throwing a brick through a shop window. B denies this but A has positive proof. For every bit of proof A comes up with B always manages to give an innocent explanation. Keep the improvisation going for as long as you can.

2 Some of the comedy in the scene comes from stating the obvious in a ridiculous way: 'The gun spat metal, a gob of metal which parted her soft tissues. I think it was then she died'. (Lines 135-6.) In pairs or small groups invent a scene in which people only say what is absolutely obvious.

3 Another comic moment is when we find out that the killer's name is Bombay Bill, also known as The Slaughterer, and that his address is Skull Lane. (Lines 112-13.) As a whole class set up a party at the annual conference for the 'Society of Those with Names Befitting Their Jobs'.

4 Underlying the comedy one can detect a few serious comments; for example, 'I have slain no-one. It was the gunmaker.' (Line 138.) Discuss what you think this comment and the one following it – 'It was the Hebrew who made the law she broke' (Line 140) – might mean. Write or improvise a scene in which someone visits another land in which something that we would consider very wrong is accepted as normal.

5 Experiment with ways of turning a 'normal' conversation into an absurd one. For example, try replacing certain key words with others that don't fit. In a conversation about school the word 'school' could be replaced by the word 'banana'. As you get used to the idea change more and more of the words while keeping the delivery and tone of the conversation 'normal'. Think back to your earlier work on tone of voice and pace in order to make it sound as if the conversation is sensible though the words being spoken are nonsense.

6 As a variant of the technique used in Question 5, try to make a conversation appear absurd and comic by using an inappropriate style of speech. Imagine, for example, if motor mechanics talked to car owners in the same way as a doctor might talk to the relatives of a dying patient.

7 Although She's Dead has a lot of comedy in it, there is something rather nightmarish about it also. What do you normally associate with the idea of 'Hell'? What, on the other hand, would be 'Hell' for you personally? Devise a scene in which a group of criminals arrive in Hell and discover that it is full of things they personally loathe the most.

JOHNSON OVER JORDAN

by J.B. Priestley

CAST (in order of appearance)

CLERK
JOHNSON
EXAMINER ONE
EXAMINER TWO
* SECRETARIES AND CLERKS

4 speaking parts. No doubling.
* non-speaking parts

Between the two World Wars British theatre took on a very conventional air. Although some of the plays written in that period are certainly masterpieces they tend to be so more because of the way they are written rather than the stories they tell or the themes they explore. This was the age of the 'well-made play'. There was little experimentation in form or style and success was measured not in terms of a play's literary quality or the originality of its ideas, but by how well it appealed to West End audiences.

J.B. Priestley was different to the run-of-the-mill playwrights of the time in many respects. While he didn't try to break away from the accepted style of writing of the time, he did try to tackle new ideas and question old ones. Underlying nearly all his plays is a message about the importance of social responsibility; he frequently lampooned and criticised the behaviour and attitudes of the businessmen who would probably have made up most of the audiences in the West End theatres. There is a down-to-earth quality in many of his characters; they seem to represent certain types of people rather than being complex personalities in their own right. Priestley's own radical background made him want audiences to ask themselves questions about the way the world was going. The fact that so much modern British theatre now addresses itself to political and social issues may largely be due to the influence of his work.

Something that interested Priestley immensely was the concept of 'Time'. A number of scientists of the period were offering various theories about the actual nature of time and Priestley, in a number of plays such as *Time and the Conways*, tried to show what the implications of these theories were in human terms.

In *Johnson Over Jordan* he explores the possibility of a kind of 'fourth dimension' in which we might exist after death. This spiritual reality is made up of images from an earthly life. Priestley might be suggesting that the key to what our lives mean rests not in our bodily presence but in the impression we leave in other people and what impression they leave in us.

The play starts with Robert Johnson's wife, children and close friends leaving his house to attend his funeral. It then switches into another dimension into which Johnson, unaware of his death, has been projected. Johnson goes on a strange journey during which he meets various characters from his past and is forced to confront his failings in life in order to appreciate the true value of his achievements and so move on to a final state of rest.

The style of the play

Although the play is constructed in a way that audiences in the 1930s were used to, the style of presentation would have been quite a novelty. Priestley's suggestions for the use of sound, light, mask and movement seem to have more similarities with the work of Strindberg than the usual drawing-room dramas or comedies of the English stage at the time. The action switches through time and space as Johnson embarks on a strange and sometimes scary journey into his own conscience. As a character he is a sort of Everyman – the typical chap – and the people he meets in this world after death are distinct stereotypes.

The extract

Johnson first appears in a tight white spotlight. He is delirious but bit by bit imagines himself to be in his office. As his vision becomes clearer to him so the lights on stage reveal it. However, the office is peopled with clerks and secretaries who go about their business in a kind of manic ballet. A voice booms over the loudspeaker issuing orders to those sitting at desks desperately trying to fill in impossibly difficult forms.

CLERK (*cutting in*]   Here's your form.

> *He hands over the form, then turns away, but this is not good enough for* JOHNSON, *who stops him, not far from one of the big office doors.*

JOHNSON [*with the remnant of his patience*]   Just a moment, please.

CLERK [*unpleasantly*]   We're busy here, you know, very busy. Listen!   5

> *He opens the nearest door, and we hear the clatter of a very large office – typewriters, adding machines, ringing of bells, etc. But now* JOHNSON *really loses his temper.*

JOHNSON [*shouting angrily*]   I don't care how busy you are. I want to know something.

CLERK [*very civil now*]   Certainly, Mr Johnson. What is it?

JOHNSON   I want to know where I am. What *is* this place?

CLERK   Central offices of the Universal Assurance and Globe   10
Loan and Finance Corporation. Where you get your money.

JOHNSON [*remembering*]   Ah – yes, of course. My money.

CLERK [*smiling*]   We all have to have money, haven't we? Can't do without that.

JOHNSON [*rather confusedly*]   No, of course not. But – the   15
trouble is, you see – well, I must have lost my memory.... I've been ill.... I was in bed – yes, in a nursing home ... doctors coming all the time ... two nurses ... everybody looking worried.... I must have wandered out some-how....   20

CLERK [*with the air of one dealing with a child*]   Quite so. Well, all you have to do is to fill in your form properly and then we give you your money. You can't get out of here until you have your money, so of course you have to stay here until you've filled in your form properly.   25

JOHNSON [*rather dubiously*]   Yes – well – that's reasonable enough. Filled in plenty of forms in my time – all kinds – [*glances at the huge form in his hand.*] Pretty elaborate sort of thing, though – isn't it? Complicated questions. Is – er – all this necessary?   30

CLERK Most certainly. You must concentrate, Mr Johnson, concentrate.

JOHNSON I'll do my best.

CLERK And our examiners will be here in a moment.

JOHNSON [*who doesn't like the sound of this*] What 35
examiners?

CLERK For the usual preliminary questions. Meanwhile, Mr Johnson, I advise you to take a good look at your form.

> *He goes out.* JOHNSON *walks slowly to the chair at the back of the desk, sits down and stares in bewilderment at the pages of complicated questions. As he stares he pulls a pipe out and sticks it into his mouth. Immediately the voice from the loud-speaker says severely: 'No smoking in the office before five-fifteen.' After giving the loud-speaker a startled glance,* JOHNSON *puts the pipe away. He tries to apply himself to the form, but now the lights change, the ballet of clerks and secretaries comes rushing in, making strange shadows, and we hear again their strident nervous music. When these clerks and secretaries have gone and the brilliant white lights pour down on the desk again, we discover that the* EXAMINERS *have arrived, and are standing one on each side of* JOHNSON, *who is still seated. They are exactly alike, these* EXAMINERS, *tall and round figures, dressed in frock-coats, with bald pink heads and round pink shaven faces and large spectacles. They carry notebooks.* JOHNSON *looks at them in astonishment touched with horror, as well he might.*

FIRST EXAMINER [*announcing himself*] First Examiner.

SECOND EXAMINER [*announcing himself*] Second Examiner. 40

FIRST EXAMINER Robert Johnson?

JOHNSON Yes.

SECOND EXAMINER [*glancing at his notes*] Born in Grantham Street, Longfield?

JOHNSON Yes. 45

FIRST EXAMINER [*reading from his notes*] Elder son of Frederick Johnson, solicitor's clerk, who for more than ten years sacrificed a number of personal comforts and pleasures in order to give you a good education?

JOHNSON [*staggered*] Yes, I suppose he did. He – was a good 50
father.

SECOND EXAMINER Did you ever thank him for those
sacrifices?

JOHNSON [*rather shamefaced*] No. And I ought to have done.

SECOND EXAMINER [*referring to his notes*] Your mother, Edith 55
Johnson, I see, died of peritonitis at a comparatively early
age. She was warned that an operation was necessary but
refused to have one in time because she was afraid of the
expense and the trouble it would cause her husband and
children. You knew that, of course? 60

JOHNSON [*deeply troubled*] No – I didn't. I – I sometimes
wondered – that's all.

FIRST EXAMINER [*glancing at his notebook, relentlessly*] And
yet you have referred to yourself at times, I see, as a good
son. 65

JOHNSON [*thoroughly uncomfortable*] I only meant – well –
we all seemed to get on together, y'know – not like some
families. They were very decent to me. I've always admitted
that. [*Hesistantly.*] As a matter of fact, I've been thinking
about all that . . . just lately. . . . I remember, just after I was 70
taken ill –

SECOND EXAMINER [*briskly*] Yes now – you were taken ill.

JOHNSON [*brightening up, for we are all proud of our
illnesses*] Yes. Quite suddenly. A most extraordinary thing
– but – 75

FIRST EXAMINER [*cutting in, ruthlessly*] You have occupied a
responsible position for some time?

JOHNSON [*bewildered and rather sulky*] Yes, I suppose so.

SECOND EXAMINER [*severely*] You are a husband – and a
father? 80

JOHNSON Yes.

FIRST EXAMINER [*severely*] What care have you taken of your
health?

JOHNSON [*apologetically*] Well – I've always tried –

FIRST EXAMINER [*ignoring him*] The heart, the lungs, the liver 85
and kidneys, the digestive system, the intestinal tract.

SECOND EXAMINER The abdominal wall must be firm – no
sagging.

FIRST EXAMINER [*who now sits on the desk, facing* JOHNSON] The
  teeth need the greatest care. Particles of decaying food 90
  lodged in dental cavities may produce a septic condition.
SECOND EXAMINER [*also sitting*] Eye-strain is common among
  sedentary workers. How often have you given yourself a
  boracic eyebath or had your sight examined?
FIRST EXAMINER Alcohol and rich starchy foods must be 95
  avoided. Have you avoided them?
SECOND EXAMINER Smoking leads to nicotine poisoning and
  may easily ruin the digestion.
FIRST EXAMINER Everywhere you go, you risk infection.
SECOND EXAMINER But the common cold, the beginning of 100
  many serious ailments, may be traced to a lack of fresh air.
FIRST EXAMINER Few of us take the trouble to walk properly.
SECOND EXAMINER Or to sit properly. You should always sit
  upright, not allowing the spine to be curved. Learn to sit
  properly. 105

> *The wretched* JOHNSON, *who has been slumped deep into
> his chair, now sharply raises himself to a more erect
> position, but it does not help him.*

FIRST EXAMINER But take care to relax. The nervous strain of
  modern life demands constant and complete relaxation.
  Loosen those tense muscles.
JOHNSON [*slumping again, but determined to protest at
  last*] Now – look here – just a minute – ! 110
SECOND EXAMINER [*very severely, rising*] Please – we have no
  time to waste.

> *The two monsters make rapid and contemptuous notes in
> their books, while* JOHNSON *regards them helplessly.*

FIRST EXAMINER You owe it yourself, to your wife and family,
  to your employer and fellow workers, to your country, to
  take sufficient exercise. 115
JOHNSON [*who mistakenly feels on safe ground here*] I've
  always enjoyed taking exercise. Tennis and golf –
SECOND EXAMINER [*very severely*] Too many middle-aged men,
  sedentary workers, imagine they can improve their physical

condition by rushing into games at the week-end, and only 120
succeed in straining their hearts.

JOHNSON [*desperately*] I've tried not to overdo it, and every
morning, if I wasn't too late, I did a few exercises in my
bedroom –

FIRST EXAMINER [*very severely*] Nearly all systems of home 125
exercises, devised by professional strong men without expert
physiological knowledge, are liable to do more harm than
good.

SECOND EXAMINER Consult your doctor first. *He* knows.

FIRST EXAMINER But the habit of flying to the doctor on every 130
trivial occasion is dangerous and must be avoided.

JOHNSON [*sinking fast now*] Look here, gentlemen, all I can
say is – I've tried to do my best.

SECOND EXAMINER [*going right up to him, in smooth deadly
tone*] Possibly. But is your best good enough? 135

FIRST EXAMINER [*with the same horrible technique*] After all,
what do you *know*?

SECOND EXAMINER [*severe again now*] How far have you tried
to acquaint yourself with the findings of chemistry, physics,
biology, ecology, astronomy, mathematics? 140

FIRST EXAMINER Ask yourself what you know about the
Mendelian Law, the Quantum Theory, Spectral analysis, or
the behaviour of Electrons and Neutrons.

SECOND EXAMINER Could you explain Freud's theory of the Id,
Marx's Surplus Value, Neo-Realism, Non-representational 145
Art, Polyphonic Music?

FIRST EXMAINER Or – give an exact account of the sequence of
events leading up to the outbreak of war in 1914?

SECOND EXAMINER [*with dangerous easiness*] You were taught
French at school? 150

JOHNSON Yes.

SECOND EXAMINER [*turning like a tiger*] Have you ever
brushed up your French?

JOHNSON [*desperately*] No, but I've always been meaning to.
Hang it! – a man can't do everything – 155

FIRST EXAMINER [*calmly and maddeningly*] A postman in
South-East London taught himself to speak eight foreign
languages fluently in his spare time.

SECOND EXAMINER [*in the same tone*] A cinema operator in Pasadena, California, recently received an honours degree in natural sciences.   160

JOHNSON [*wearily, almost brokenly*] I know, I know. And good luck to them. But as I told you –

FIRST EXAMINER [*very severely*] Kindly tell us what we ask you to tell us. We have no time now for general conversation.   165 You have two children?

JOHNSON [*brightening up, for this may let him out*] Yes. A boy and a girl.

SECOND EXAMINER You are fond of them?

JOHNSON [*indignantly*] Of course I am.   170

FIRST EXAMINER What serious thought have you ever given to their education, to their mental development, to their emotional and spiritual life?

SECOND EXAMINER They are the citizens of the future, the inheritors of a great empire –   175

JOHNSON I know, I know. I've often thought of that.

SECOND EXAMINER [*pressing him*] Really thought about it, or merely, after an unnecessarily heavy meal accompanied by alcohol, congratulated yourself that these children were an extension of your own ego?   180

FIRST EXAMINER You have helped to bring them into the world, but what kind of world have you brought them into?

JOHNSON [*hastily, hoping he is now on firmer ground*] Oh – well – I've no illusions about that –

SECOND EXAMINER [*angrily*] We are not asking you about your   185 illusions. For many years now you have had a vote?

JOHNSON [*still hoping*] Yes, and I've always used it – not like some chaps –

FIRST EXAMINER But how much of your time and serious attention have been given to the problems that must be   190 studied by a wise member of the electorate?

SECOND EXAMINER For example, the Gold Standard as against an artificial currency based on the balance of trade. The relation between nationalism and Tariffs. The fallacy of colonial exploitation.   195

FIRST EXAMINER What account of any value could you give of the political significance of minorities in Central Europe, the importance of the Ukraine in European affairs, the success or failure of Stalin's second Five Year Plan?

SECOND EXAMINER   Could you define accurately Fascism?   200

FIRST EXAMINER   National Socialism?

SECOND EXAMINER   Russian Communism?

JOHNSON [*a rebel at last, jumping up*]   No. Could you? [*As they do not reply, but make notes.*] I might as well tell you, I've had enough of this. Who are you, anyhow? [*As they do   205 not reply, but look at each other significantly.*] I don't even know why I'm here. Loss of memory – or something. No reason why I should stay.

FIRST EXAMINER [*ignoring this outburst*]   Your form, please.

He takes the form, hastily makes some marks on it, then hands it back.

JOHNSON [*angrily*]   I don't want the thing.   210

JOHNSON *throws the form on the table and sits sulking. The two* EXAMINERS *look at the form, then at him, give a nod to each other, and go off through one of the big office doors.*

JOHNSON   I'm not staying, y'know. Why should I? I didn't want to come here. Keep your money.

But the EXAMINER *has gone.* JOHNSON *sits slumped in his chair behind the desk, a sulky rebel.*

Understanding the text

1 List three things in the extract that suggest the scene is not taking place in the real world.

2 What sort of person do you imagine Johnson to be? Write brief notes describing any faults and qualities that you think he has. (For example, he seems to be quite impatient at first.) Add what you think his main likes, dislikes, hobbies and habits might be (judging from this first introduction.)

3 The Examiners disturb Johnson with their questions. Which appear to worry him the most? What might this suggest about his character?

4 Johnson looks rather small and foolish in this scene. Apart from the difficult questions he is asked, what other things make him appear so?

Producing the scene

1 Write out a list of all the sound effects actually demanded in the script and suggest more if you think they are appropriate. Experiment with ways of making some of the sounds.

2 In places the stage directions suggest music. Could you suggest any music you know which might be suitable? Actually recording a sound track for this scene could be an unusual and interesting project.

3 How might you create the strange shadows suggested in the long stage direction, and generally make the 'office' seem nightmarish by using the lighting equipment you have available? If you know of the existence of other types of lights that you could hire, consider them also.

4 Finding two people who look exactly alike to play the Examiners could be a considerable problem. One solution which would also add to the strangeness of the scene might be to make identical masks.
  • Jot down some ideas about the type of characters the examiners seem to have.
  • Design a caricature which reflects their attitudes.

5 By acting out the scene, try to find ways for the Examiners to make Johnson feel small and uncomfortable by the way they move around him during the 'interrogation'. Write a stage direction which describes how they should move.

6 Do you think the Examiners ought to ask their questions at a steady, even pace all the way through the scene, or should they increase the pace? Experiment with both methods and note the different qualities of each before making your final choice.

7 At the end of the scene Johnson starts to stick up for himself by shouting at the Examiners. However, they have already gone and so the gesture is rather wasted. How could you make Johnson's rebellion look totally futile on stage? Consider how you could achieve this through lighting, position on stage, gesture and facial expression.

Further development

1 You might have heard it said that your whole life flashes in front of you when you're drowning. In groups of about six improvise, at breakneck speed and off the tops of your heads, someone's life from birth to death.

2 In *Johnson Over Jordan*, Johnson re-encounters several characters from his past life whom he has cause to remember. In groups of four or five (more if you think you can manage) prepare a programme set in the next

world called 'Robert Johnson, This WAS Your Life!' You may choose to introduce only two or three characters in the programme.

3 Write or improvise a story in which a person who has died must resolve a piece of 'unfinished business' on earth before she is allowed to move on to her final resting place.

4 Get into pairs and label yourselves A and B. A starts a spontaneous improvisation by taking Johnson's lines, 'I've been ill . . . I must have wandered out somehow. . .' (Lines 17-20) Work on this for no more than one minute and then start a new scene in which B says these lines. Generate as many different quick-fire scenes as you can always using this same starting line. Which one struck you as having most potential? Try to script it or develop it through further improvisation.

5 Working in groups of three improvise an interrogation session in which the aim is not so much to find out information from the 'victim' as to confuse and frustrate her totally. Try to make use of the following techniques:

- varying the speed of the questions
- moving round the person
- changing the tone and volume of your voices
- changing the characters of the interrogators

and do anything else that will make it difficult for the victim to concentrate.

After a few minutes choose a new person to be the victim so you all have a chance to play both roles. Talk about both how you personally felt about the experience and about ways of turning that into a piece of carefully prepared theatre afterwards.

6 Improvise a scene in which a number of ghosts are returning home, wherever that might be, after a hard night's haunting. How could you develop the idea that they have been able to see and touch living people without being seen themselves? What would make it a 'hard night's haunting'?

7 If you have access to sound and lighting equipment devise a way of using it to produce an 'atmosphere' which could be used at the opening of a play to suggest something eerie.

THE SPANISH TRAGEDY

by Thomas Kyd

CAST (in order of appearance)

KING
VICEROY
HIERONIMO
DUKE OF CASTILE
ANDREA
REVENGE

6 speaking parts. No doubling.

Written around 1589 in the reign of Queen Elizabeth I, *The Spanish Tragedy* captures a great deal of the fiery spirit of the age. On the one hand it reflects fascination with the poetic possibilities of words. Elizabethan audiences were good listeners and enjoyed language which had been finely crafted. They were similarly enthralled by the lives and adventures of the rich and powerful – people they saw as holding a higher station in life than themselves. On the other hand one could say that plays such as this reflect a viciousness and a glee at seeing the high and mighty fall tragically and dramatically off their pedestals.

As well as being an age of new discoveries and brave deeds (think of Sir Francis Drake and Sir Walter Raleigh) it was also an age of political intrigue and dark dealings. The violence of the play reflects the violence of the time. Kyd himself was imprisoned for treacherous and heretical writing which he claimed was actually the work of Christopher Marlowe, another playwright of the time. Whilst Kyd was in prison Marlowe was stabbed to death in a fight in a tavern in Deptford. The exact relationship between the two writers and what parts they played in the ruthless power struggles of the age remain a mystery.

In *The Spanish Tragedy* (and many other plays of its time) the balance of justice and honour has been upset by the committing of a bloody crime. Those affected by this crime try to restore the balance in a totally ruthless and uncompromising way. They seek violent revenge that can only lead to tragedy.

The plot

The play opens with the appearance of the ghost of Andrea, a Spanish soldier who has been killed in a war against Portugal. Andrea was killed by Balthazar who was taken prisoner for the deed by Andrea's friend, Horatio.

Andrea's ghost has been allowed out of the Underworld with the character of Revenge in order to see how his mistress, Bel-imperia, will deal with the murderer of her lover. Balthazar becomes friendly with Bel-imperia's brother, Lorenzo, and the two of them try to persuade Bel-imperia to accept Balthazar's advances. Bel-imperia, however, has fallen in love with the brave Horatio – a choice she feels her dead lover would not object to. Balthazar and Lorenzo murder Horatio and – in the midst of many other twists of the plot – Bel-imperia plots vengeance on them both with Horatio's father, Hieronimo. Vengeance is achieved when Hieronimo and Bel-imperia persuade their two enemies to act in a tragic play in the presence of Lorenzo's father (the Duke), Balthazar's father (the Viceroy) and the King of Spain. In the course of the play the two men are murdered – apparently as part of the action of the play, but in fact for real. Bel-imperia kills herself and, determined not to reveal whose plan it was under torture, Hieronimo bites his own tongue off before killing himself and the Duke.

The extract

This is the last scene of the play. The audience of Hieronimo's play have realised that the murders were real. In a long and impassioned speech, Hieronimo has explained why he has sought such a dreadful vengeance. The scene should be played with an intensity of emotion and anger on the part of all the characters at the way their comfortable world has collapsed. This is then contrasted with the cold venom of the dead Andrea who, pleased that justice has been done, looks forward to greeting his friends in the Underworld and seeing his enemies condemned to an 'endless tragedy'.

KING   O hearken, Viceroy! Hold, Hieronimo!
　　Brother, my nephew and thy son are slain!
VICEROY   We are betrayed! my Balthazar is slain!
　　Break ope the doors, run, save Hieronimo.

They break in, and hold HIERONIMO.

　　Hieronimo, do but inform the king of these events;　　　5
　　Upon mine honour thou shalt have no harm.
HIERONIMO   Viceroy, I will not trust thee with my life,
　　Which I this day have offered to my son.
　　Accursed wretch,
　　Why stayest thou him that was resolved to die?　　　10
KING   Speak, traitor; damned, bloody murderer, speak!
　　For now I have thee I will make thee speak –
　　Why hast thou done this undeserving deed?
VICEROY   Why hast thou murdered my Balthazar?
CASTILE   Why hast thou butchered both my children thus?　　15
HIERONIMO   O, good words!
　　As dear to me was my Horatio
　　As yours, or yours, or yours, my lord, to you.
　　My guiltless son was by Lorenzo slain,
　　And by Lorenzo and that Balthazar　　　20
　　Am I at last revenged thoroughly,
　　Upon whose souls may heavens be yet avenged
　　With greater far than these afflictions.
CASTILE   But who were thy confederates in this?
VICEROY   That was thy daughter Bel-imperia;　　　25
　　For by her hand my Balthazar was slain:
　　I saw her stab him.
KING　　　　　　　　Why speak'st thou not?
HIERONIMO   What lesser liberty can kings afford
　　Than harmless silence? then afford it me:
　　Sufficeth I may not, nor I will not tell thee.　　　30
KING   Fetch forth the tortures.
　　Traitor as thou art, I'll make thee tell.
HIERONIMO　　　　　　　　　　Indeed,
　　Thou may'st torment me, as his wretched son
　　Hath done in murdering my Horatio,

But never shalt thou force me to reveal   35
The thing which I have vowed inviolate.
And therefore in despite of all thy threats,
Pleased with their deaths, and eased with their revenge,
First take my tongue, and afterwards my heart.

He bites out his tongue

KING   O monstrous resolution of a wretch!   40
See, Viceroy, he hath bitten forth his tongue
Rather than to reveal what we required.
CASTILE   Yet can he write.
KING   And if in this he satisfy us not,
We will devise th'extremest kind of death   45
That ever was invented for a wretch.

Then he makes signs for a knife to mend his pen

CASTILE   O, he would have a knife to mend his pen.
VICEROY   Here; and advise thee that thou write the troth.
KING   Look to my brother! save Hieronimo!

He with a knife stabs the DUKE *and himself*

What age hath ever heard such monstrous deeds?   50
My brother, and the whole succeeding hope
That Spain expected after my decease!
Go bear his body hence, that we may mourn
The loss of our beloved brother's death;
That he may be entombed, whate'er befall: 55
I am the next, the nearest, last of all.
VICEROY   And thou Don Pedro, do the like for us;
Take up our hapless son, untimely slain:
Set me with him, and he with woeful me,
Upon the main-mast of a ship unmanned,   60
And let the wind and tide haul me along
To Scylla's barking and untamed gulf,
Or to the loathsome pool of Acheron,
To weep my want for my sweet Balthazar:
Spain hath no refuge for a Portingale.   65

line 48   *advise thee*   take care

The trumpets sound a dead march, the KING OF SPAIN *mourning after his brother's body, and the* VICEROY OF PORTINGALE *bearing the body of his son*

Act IV, Scene v
Ghost [of ANDREA] *and* REVENGE

ANDREA   Ay, now my hopes have end in their effects,
When blood and sorrow finish my desires:
Horatio murdered in his father's bower,
Vile Serberine by Pedringano slain,
False Pedringano hanged by quaint device,   70
Fair Isabella by herself misdone,
Prince Balthazar by Bel-imperia stabbed,
The Duke of Castile and his wicked son
Both done to death by old Hieronimo,
My Bel-imperia fallen as Dido fell,   75
And good Hieronimo slain by himself:
Ay, these were spectacles to please my soul.
Now will I beg at lovely Proserpine,
That, by the virtue of her princely doom,
I may consort my friends in pleasing sort,   80
And on my foes work just and sharp revenge.
I'll lead my friend Horatio through those fields
Where never-dying wars are still inured:
I'll lead fair Isabella to that train
Where pity weeps but never feeleth pain: 85
I'll lead my Bel-imperia to those joys
That vestal virgins and fair queens possess;
I'll lead Hieronimo where Orpheus plays,
Adding sweet pleasure to eternal days.
But say, Revenge, for thou must help, or none,   90
Against the rest how shall my hate be shown?
REVENGE   This hand shall hale them down to deepest hell,
Where none but Furies, bugs and tortures dwell.

line 79   *doom*   judgement
line 80   *consort*   accompany

ANDREA   Then, sweet Revenge, do this at my request;
  Let me be judge, and doom them to unrest: 95
  Let loose poor Tityus from the vulture's gripe,
  And let Don Cyprian supply his room;
  Place Don Lorenzo on Ixion's wheel,
  And let the lover's endless pains surcease –
  Juno forgets old wrath, and grants him ease;   100
  Hang Balthazar about Chimaera's neck,
  And let him there bewail his bloody love,
  Repining at our joys that are above;
  Let Serberine go roll the fatal stone,
  And take from Sisyphus his endless moan;   105
  False Pedringano for his treachery,
  Let him be dragged through boiling Acheron,
  And there live, dying still in endless flames,
  Blaspheming gods and all their holy names.
REVENGE   Then haste we down to meet thy friends and foes: 110
  To place thy friends in ease, the rest in woes.
  For here, though death hath end their misery,
  I'll there begin their endless tragedy.

    Exeunt

Understanding the text

1 The scene is full of violent words and phrases: 'loathsome', 'untamed', 'wretch', 'th' extremest form of death', and so on. Pick out as many such examples as you can. Why do you think the writer uses so much descriptive language of this sort?

2 A feature of the 'revenge tragedy' is the way in which the balance of justice and honour is restored. Those who have profited from crime and injustice are made to pay for it. Who, in this extract, find themselves in this position? Why is this and how is it achieved in each case?

3 Look carefully at Andrea's first speech. What do we learn about the whole story from this? What, do you think, is the purpose of having such a speech at the end of this play?

4 There are many classical references in this extract; that is, names or phrases which come from older stories and works of literature. Pick out at

least three such references. What effect do they have on you? What effect do you suppose they would have had on an Elizabethan audience? Suggest a few reasons as to how and why the audience's appreciation of these references has changed?

Producing the scene

1 What sort of atmosphere do you think should be created in this scene – ghoulish, violent, sinister, angry? How could you use lights and sound effects to help build such an atmosphere?

2 Design the costume and make-up for either (or both) the ghost of Andrea and/or Revenge.

3 Imagine you are a publicity agency which has been commissioned to produce a poster for a production of *The Spanish Tragedy*. Your design should reflect the atmosphere and plot of the play. How can you achieve a balance so as to capture the horror and goriness without making it look like a cheap video nasty? If you feel you couldn't do your ideas justice by drawing them, you could describe what the poster should contain by use of words and diagrams.

4 How would you solve the problem of the stage direction *He bites out his tongue*? Consider the advantages and disadvantages of the following methods:

- the action is suggested by some stylised action or movement
- a fake tongue and stage blood are used to produce a gory effect.

Can you think of another way? If possible try out various techniques to see which one works best for you.

5 The pace, emotion and atmosphere change directly after the Duke is stabbed (line 49). Look carefully at the lines leading up to this (lines 44–9) and the ones immediately following. What advice would you give to the actor playing the King about how to deliver the speech after the stabbing, bearing in mind this change of pace? In pairs, work as actor and director to test out possible alternatives.

6 Read the scene through again and try to paraphrase one of the longer speeches in your own language. (The King's speech after the stabbing would be a good choice.) This technique can be a useful way of helping you to understand both what is happening in a scene like this and the emotions behind what the characters are saying. Acting out such scenes in your own words may also have disadvantages for you. Try acting the scene out in this way, concentrating mainly on what is being said, and note down the advantages and disadvantages of the technique.

Further development

1 In pairs, improvise a scene in which a servant who witnessed these events is describing them to another servant. The two then speculate on what will happen next to these noblemen. Will there be a 'cover-up'? Will it affect their lives in any way?

2 Imagine Hieronimo didn't bite his tongue out and die, but is, eventually, taken to court for the double murder of Lorenzo and the Duke of Castile. The night before sentence is passed, Hieronimo dreams of some of the people who have been involved in or affected by the tragedy. Some are living, some dead. How would they appear in his dream? What would their attitude be and what would they say? Don't try to restrict your improvisation to characters actually in the story but invent some others who may, nevertheless, be affected by it. You could refer back to the summary of the plot on page 73 to help you with this activity.

3 By appealing to Lorenzo's and Balthazar's big egos, Hieronimo lures them both into his deadly play. Devise a short play of your own in which a person's flawed character leads her to a nasty end.

4 Portraying ghosts by putting white sheets over your heads is unavoidably comical. In pairs or small groups use movement and possibly your own sounds to create a theatrical image that more successfully captures something sinister and supernatural. If you have the facilities for using sound and lighting equipment, experiment with that also.

5 As was mentioned previously, revenge was seen as a means of re-establishing a balance after a wrong had been done. Use this notion as the basis of a piece of written or improvised work of your own. It should be clear in your work exactly how the original balance was upset and in what way revenge will restore it.

6 It may seem strange at first to have a character called 'Revenge'. However, writers often turn ideas into personalities; the technique is called 'personification'. Consider, for example, the characters of 'Old Father Time' or 'Death'. In small groups choose an 'idea' which could be presented as an actual character. What traits would the character have? How would she move and talk and what would her gestures be? Devise a scene in which such a character appears.

THE LUCKY ONES

by Tony Marchant

CAST (in order of appearance)

DAVE

TIMOTHY

DEBBIE

JOE

LAWRENCE

5 speaking parts. No doubling.

Writing plays about contemporary issues is a dangerous business. Theatres are often worried about putting anything on that seems 'political' or critical of a society which they rely on for business. Another problem for the writer is that if the play is specifically about one aspect of current life, then it is unlikely to be performed much in the future because it might be seen as irrelevant. Fortunately, there are some theatre companies that will take a chance and put on such plays, and sometimes they are also published, which improves their chance of being performed more widely.

Whether Tony Marchant's play will still be performed in ten years' time remains to be seen. With its underlying theme of mass unemployment it is very much a play of its time. However, one can see in it universal themes and problems; for example, the question of how to get on in the world; does one stand up and fight for one's rights or keep out of the way and hope that one will be rewarded for doing so?

The Lucky Ones is set in the basement of an office building. The four main characters are clearing out boxes of old files. It is a boring and mindless job for which they are paid little. Dave is resentful of the way in which the company treats them as cheap labour. He likens life to a vending machine which won't give anything after you've put your money in: 'Some people smash the machine to bits but they get arrested. Some people are luckier and manage to negotiate a packet of Wrigley's which is not what they wanted at all, but they're thankful for whatever the machine is kind enough to let them have.' He is supported to some extent by

80

Debbie who, as a girl, has the additional problem of being leered at by some of the managers and seen as an object rather than a person. Timothy has a different approach. 'Be acceptable' is his advice to Joe who has just joined the firm and is hoping to make enough money to get married and settle down with his girlfriend, Sandra.

The test of loyalty to the firm comes when the young staff are asked to act as waiters outside office hours at an evening presentation to the firm's managing director.

The style of the play

In a sense *The Lucky Ones* has a quite traditional style in that it tells a story in a straightforward, sequenced way. At the beginning the characters are introduced and the main incident occurs, we then see how the characters react to the incident, and finally see what happens to them because of the way they reacted. It is a 'naturalistic' type of play in that it tries to capture on stage the words and actions of recognisable characters in a believable way. The language of the play is similarly realistic and attempts to reflect how many young people talk to each other when they are together.

The extract

This is a scene from the middle of the play. Dave, Debbie, Joe and Tim have already been asked to contribute towards buying a present for their boss, Mr Gulley. Now they have been asked to act as waiters at the presentation. They divide into those who want to take a 'militant' line in an attempt to preserve their dignity, and those who will go along with the plan because they think that is the safer and wiser thing to do.

Scene five

DAVE, JOE, DEBBIE *and* TIM *are in the middle of a conversation.*

DAVE Well, it's a liberty if you ask me. Talk about wringing out the last few drops. He'll come down and give us a fitting for a ball and chain next. First we have to do a collection for a presentation we ain't even invited to . . .

TIMOTHY   You're invited now . . .   5

DAVE   What – as a barman – fixing gin and tonics for our
poxy senior management and their wives so's they can have
a jolly fine evening at our expense? More ice please young
man. Don't you work here as the lift attendant or
something? Very nice little turn out wouldn't you say?   10
Cheers. I'd rather be a store detective for War on Want
sometimes, I tell you.

TIMOTHY   At least you'll be there. None of the other clerks
will be.

DEBBIE   It wasn't exactly RSVP with gold lettering though, was   15
it? Not a hint of you are cordially invited, Mr Gulley
requests the pleasure of your company. Wasn't even would
you, could you, please, I'd be grateful. No nothing like that.
Quick visit five o'clock last night to inform us that he wants
us to wait on them hand and foot. Only his euphemism was   20
giving our assistance. Token mention of his appreciation.

TIMOTHY   And a not so token mention that we'd be getting
paid for it.

DEBBIE   Ever heard of that old-fashioned cliché called the
principle of the thing.   25

DAVE   It ain't even time and a half.

JOE   I need all the money I can get hold of at the moment.
Sandra says that for the honeymoon she wants to go to
Tenerife. And the reception's going to be a four course sit-
down with wine included, followed by a group – spot prizes,   30
special requests and me and Sandra out on the floor for the
first dance. [*Pause*.] They might give us a tip or something.
Like when they have a whip-round for the coach driver.

DAVE   What coach driver?

JOE   Well, generally like. On the way back from wherever   35
you've been. After the singing.

DAVE   Singing?

JOE   Yeah. *When the Saints Go Marching In*. [*Pause*.] All
together. [*Pause*.] Might be like that next week.

DAVE   Oh yeah – I can just see it now. We'll all get together in   40
a big circle at the end of the evening and do the hokey-
kokey.

   Pause.

We don't want tipping – we want our self-respect.

DEBBIE Won't get much of that when you're having to ask some old berk's wife if she'd like a cherry in her advocaat or coleslaw with her chicken leg. 45

TIMOTHY What are you going to do then – stop watering the office plants in protest, set fire to the blotting paper and call it industrial espionage or write a letter of complaint to the staff magazine? Maybe you'll get some placards and march up and down outside Lawrence's office. 50

DAVE [going deliberately over the top to compete with TIM and hopefully bait him] Yeah, we're going on a go-slow; black the work, withdraw our good-will, picket the stationery cupboard and the executive bog, stand by our entitlements. 55 We're not going to stand for it. In other words, Tim old fruit, we're going to say no. In big letters. Is that simple enough for you?

TIMOTHY I'll hold your coat. [Pause.] If one isn't there next week, one is invisible. Not sensible at all. Getting noticed is. 60 Very.

DEBBIE Like a pet dog gets noticed.

TIMOTHY Pet dogs get fed. Stray ones get put down.

DAVE Timothy – don't be a bottle job, a wash out, a wally. Don't be the vulture's pickings, the dog's dinner. Know your 65 rights. Don't let your rights go out of the window for the sake of a pat on the head. Dignity. Solidarity. Victory. Stand up and speak out.

LAWRENCE has appeared at the door unnoticed at the end of DAVE's speech.

LAWRENCE Stirring stuff David. When's the battle taking place. Agincourt? 70

DAVE I .. er ... I was just giving Tim a bit of advice Mr Lawrence – useful tips when buying your Christmas turkey.

LAWRENCE Really. I've just bought this down for next week. [It is a bar steward's white jacket.] Could only get hold of 75 one for the time being. I don't know which one of you it'll fit. But you'll be properly kitted out in the end. Don't worry about that.

TIMOTHY   Dave – I don't know if it's slipped your sieve-like mind at all – but didn't you have a few queries about next 80 week.

Pause.

LAWRENCE   I'm all ears, as Prince Charles would say.
DAVE   Well . . . the presentation in the evening . . . the function . . . you want us . . . me to work behind the bar . . . serving. 85
LAWRENCE   I still do. An expert on drink such as yourself is going to be indispensable.
DAVE   And Debbie supervising the buffet.
LAWRENCE   A running cold buffet of cooked hams, chicken breast, silverside, home made quiche, various salad mixes, 90 even one with walnuts in it, chicken liver paté, garlic paté, a full selection of cheeses, smoked salmon – Canadian – canapes, potted shrimps, avocado prawn, smoked mackerel, trout, cheese dip, fresh cream gateaux and the perennial sausage rolls. Lots of lovely dishes and I'm sure you'll be the 95 loveliest, Debbie. [*Pause.*] You'll be free to take home with you whatever's left.
DAVE   I think, you see . . .
LAWRENCE   [*interrupting*]   Not getting butterflies or cement mixers or whatever are you? There aren't many that I could 100 trust enough to put on the front line so to speak. I'm sure you'll do justice to the occasion. I know you will. And as far as the etiquette business goes . . .
DAVE   Something   else   . . .   I   wanted   to   talk   about, Mr Lawrence. Me and Debbie . . . I don't know about Joe 105 . . . was thinking, not just thinking, saying as well . . . didn't think it was . . . the idea of doing . . . didn't seem what we would have decided . . . for us, I mean ourselves . . . on our own, of our own accord . . . the presentation . . . in the evening . . . agreeing . . . 110
LAWRENCE   I'm afraid you're making about as much sense as a drunken polar bear.
DAVE   Our job . . . working here . . . it's different . . . that's all we do . . . supposed to . . . normally. What we've been asked

that night . . . not the same as what's normal . . . supposed 115
to be working here . . . not the same.

LAWRENCE   You've got a bogey on the side of your nose,
David.

TIMOTHY *laughs.*

LAWRENCE   Only joking. Now what was all that again – you
must think I'm terribly slow on the uptake, I think my ears 120
might be full of wax. [*Proferring the side of his head to*
DAVID.] Can you see anything? And I hope you're not going
to say you can see out through to the other side. Either I'm
not listening or you're not communicating. Which d'you
think? 125

DAVE   What I meant to say Mr Lawrence . . . about what you
want . . .

DEBBIE   We don't want to work as waiters and waitresses next
Thursday. We don't think it's fair.

TIMOTHY   Don't include me in that. 130

Pause.

LAWRENCE   Looks like . . . we've got an insurrection. A mutiny
on board. Am I the one you've decided to make walk the
plank or what?

Pause – no response.

Bone of contention seems to concern your appreciation of
the conception of what's fair – that right? 135

DEBBIE   Wouldn't it be possible for you to get someone else to
do it Mr Lawrence?

LAWRENCE   More waiters and waitresses you mean? [*Pause.*]
On the registers of numerous employment agencies –
experienced, efficient, trained professional and eminently 140
suitable. But I wanted something much more than that, you
see. I thought there was a better way, I really did. To my
mind there's a very large distinction between yourselves and
the waiters and waitress you thought you were going to be
next Thursday. For a start, you were asked for, wanted – 145
very much so. Because I knew you wouldn't let me down, I

knew you'd be a credit to me the department and yourselves. It was a vote of confidence with the best will in the world – not a case of who can we rope in. And that's important for me to make you understand that your 150 presence there is going to be more than just a functional one. If you thought you were just being asked to turn up to pass the peanuts and pour the gin, then I'd be very disappointed in your estimation of me and what I'm about. It wouldn't be fair, to use your word. 155

DEBBIE   What else will we be there for then, Mr Lawrence?

LAWRENCE   Well, on a practical level of course you would be helping to make the evening a success, as you help to make the firm a success, by working here. I don't normally go in for platitudes, but you are part of a team here, albeit junior 160 members of that team. So wouldn't it be nice if that sense of being part of the firm, of the team, could be reflected in your helping to muck in on Thursday? A symbol of the kind of spirit we try to engender here of people working together, for each other. Next week will be a celebration of twenty- 165 five years of that spirit. Your refusing to co-operate would sour it. An extra-curricular contribution to Gulley and Co, rather than your normal nine to five one. And I think Mr Gulley is entitled to some small measure of appreciation. After all, he does pay our wages. [*Pause.*] Of course no one 170 is holding a gun to your head or threatening you with thirty lashes for insubordination. This is England, 1982. But probationary reports and promotion markings don't write themselves you know. Attitude – that's the thing.

DEBBIE   We're not trying to sabotage the evening Mr Lawrence 175 or insult Mr Gulley, I thought the collection would have proved that.

LAWRENCE   But I suppose it just goes against your religious beliefs to have anything to do with the firm after five o'clock, to be helpful and approachable only when it says so 180 in your contract of employment.

TIMOTHY   I'm quite looking forward to it myself. I won't be washing my hair that night or watching *Crossroads*.

DEBBIE   We won't be there on an equal basis will we?

LAWRENCE   So what's new – you're not here on an equal basis   185
five days a week. Anyway. I thought I'd explained that
aspect of it just now. When you go into a shop – do you
think the person giving you your newspaper or mascara or
box of tampons or whatever is some form of inferior
species? Of course you don't – unless your sensibilities are   190
warped. [*Pause.*] OK – so you're not being asked to indulge
in dry sherries and the joys of social intercourse but neither
are you going to be treated like Millwall supporters with
syphilis.

TIMOTHY   Sweating in the engine room as opposed to standing   195
on the deck.

DEBBIE   The point is though Mr Lawrence – we'll just be there
to help other people enjoy themselves and clear up after 'em
when they've finished. They'll be no celebration of the firm's
anniversary for us – not a proper one anyway. Being an   200
integral part of the spirit of the whole occasion. I mean, it
sounds very nice – but it's hard for us, me anyway – to
appreciate. It seems a bit like that fairy story about admiring
the king's new clothes. You know the one where he ain't
wearing nothing at all.   205

JOE   Danny Kaye sung a song about it.

DEBBIE   You see, I always thought that joining in meant . . .
well, what is sounds like . . . joining in.

LAWRENCE   Well, I don't think we need to make a philo-
sophical issue out of it – or create a maze of excuses. The   210
question remains – either you want to be constructive or
you don't. Abuse my trust or vindicate it. [*Pause.*] You're
being very silent David – seen your reservations put into
legitimate perspective now have you? Yes? No? Don't
know?   215

DAVE   What Debbie said . . . a lot in common with that. Not
the same as not caring though. I think I might be babysitting
for me sister next Thursday. She lives in Ilford. I have to get
a 25 from Stratford.

LAWRENCE   I would really like to go away from here feeling   220
that apart from Tim there was some kind of commitment
and interest that went beyond salary – which I think is due

for review next month, is it not? [*Pause.*] What about Joe –
prepared to put yourself out, start off on the right note and
show me that the firm's taken on a winner?   225

JOE No, I don't mind actually. Broaden my working experience won't it and . . . help me develop me office skills . . .
like communication . . . in a social environment. Showing
the right attitude – be an asset like. Only thing is though –
I'm a bit accident prone. Last do I went to I got an olive   230
stuck up me nose. That was just before I opened this bottle
of Pomagne – the cork hit this woman right in the eye, made
her false teeth fall out . . . into the coleslaw. I had to leave
early. I'm sure I'll be all right next Thursday though.

LAWRENCE How reassuring. Remember earlier on you were   235
talking about what's fair. Would your definition of fair
include the use of the democratic process, abiding by the
majority decision for the good of the community and all
that. Would it?

    DAVE *and* DEBBIE *both shrug, nod.*

Funny you should say that because if I've got my sums right   240
and a fair and democratic vote took place, it would be two
against two with me having the casting vote and conse-
quently next Thursday would be graced by both your
presences.

DEBBIE We also believe in freedom of choice Mr Lawrence.   245

LAWRENCE Let me put your freedom of choice into perspective. I was talking about this being England, 1982. Last
week, personnel had 250 applications for two vacant clerical
posts they advertised. Amazing isn't it? Steady, decent jobs
are rare things today. You're in very fortunate positions,   250
you're what's known as the lucky ones. Plenty of people
anxious to be where you are now, to push you off the perch.
250. 250 applications for two posts. Employers have
freedom of choice at the moment – bags of it. [*Pause.*]
Having a job today, especially for young people – well, it's   255
like having a life raft to hold onto in a very cold, hostile sea
– something to cling onto desperately. Only fools would

want to do something that might jeopardise their tenuous
grip on the life raft, see their fingers being prised away and
find themselves stranded in an ocean of nothing. An ocean   260
of unemployment. And there'd be nowhere else to go believe
me – not even for bright young sparks like yourselves.
Sobering thought isn't it? And of course that makes it so
much more crucial that you please your employers. You'd
do well to bear that in mind and start looking over your   265
shoulders. Let me know when you've seen the light. Cheers.

He goes out.

DAVE   Happy birthday Gulley & Co.
TIMOTHY [*who has put on the bar steward's jacket*]   How's it
look?
DEBBIE   Looks like trouble.   270

Understanding the text

1 Compare Timothy and Dave's attitude to the extra work they are being
asked to do. Look, for example, at comments like:
   TIMOTHY   If one isn't there next week, one is invisible. Not
      sensible at all. Getting noticed is.
   DAVE   Don't let your rights go out of the window for the sake of
      a pat on the head.
Divide a sheet of paper into two and list as many comments like those
above as you can in the appropriate columns.
2 What difference is there between the way Dave talks to Timothy and the
way he talks to Lawrence? What does this tell us about Dave?
3 Lawrence puts a number of reasons forward for wanting the young staff
to help at the party. Try to list all the reasons he gives. Which do you
think would be the most important to him personally?
4 This is a very 'verbal' scene. People say a great deal, but after Lawrence
comes in much of that they say seems careful and guarded as if they're not
really saying what they mean. Try to summarise the attitudes of each of
the characters and say who you think has most to gain and most to lose
through the way they deal with the situation.

Producing the scene

1 Design a set which would reflect the boring nature of the job the young staff are doing in the basement. What furniture and colour scheme would you use? Try to make your design and notes as detailed as possible.

2 How could the actors use their voices to reflect the different backgrounds and aspirations of the characters they are playing? Imagine you are auditioning for one of the parts. Choose no more than six lines and rehearse them on your own, developing what you consider to be an appropriate accent and tone of voice. Find another member of the group who has chosen the same character and compare your methods and results.

3 Look at the moment when Lawrence first enters. Act out this entrance and see if you can achieve a laugh from the audience by the way you position the characters at this moment and the timing of the actual entrance.

4 What advice would you give to the actors as to how they should react to the entrance of Lawrence in order to show both their feelings towards him and each other? Act out the entrance scene again and freeze after Lawrence's line 'When's the battle taking place?' (Line 69.) Allow each character to speak aloud one thought about Dave, Debbie and Lawrence. Replay the scene a third time and see if it is possible to 'choreograph' the facial expressions and glances in order to make these secret thoughts obvious to an audience.

5 Look at Debbie's last line and, in groups of four, pose for a still photograph. How could the positioning indicate what might happen next? Experiment with changing people's positions so that they suggest various alternatives.

6 Discuss what attitude you think the audience should have towards both the characters and the forthcoming party at the end of this scene. What do you personally feel about the situation that the young people have been put in here?

Further development

1 In groups of three invent a situation in which A wants B to do something. B is openly opposed to this but C tries to keep the peace.

2 Lawrence tells the others that the firm had received 250 applications for two posts. In pairs, improvise an interview in which Lawrence, or a character like him, is interviewing someone like Dave who doesn't really like the look of the job but needs it.

3 Lawrence tries to persuade the others to 'toe the line' but underlying his persuasion are veiled threats. In pairs, improvise a scene in which someone is persuading someone else to do something, but the more they resist, the more the persuasion becomes menacing.

4 Act out the scene at the presentation party. Does Dave take his revenge? If so, how? (Of course, if you want to know what really happens you'll have to read the whole play!)

5 'You're in very fortunate positions, you're what's known as the lucky ones.' (Line 250.) Do you think they are lucky? What do you think Dave, Debbie, Joe and Timothy are sacrificing in order to keep their jobs? People on strike often face a dilemma – do they preserve their 'self-respect' at the risk of being 'fools' who 'jeopardise their tenuous grip on the life raft', or should they 'get noticed' in the way Timothy suggests. Write or prepare an improvisation telling a story which explores such a dilemma. (Your improvisation does not necessarily have to be about a strike.)

6 *The Lucky Ones* is quite unusual in that it deals with some of the problems faced by young people. What other difficult situations do young people face which you think might make a good subject for a play? List the possibilities and try to tie a number of them together in a written or improvised story.

7 As a whole class create an instant 'waxwork' representation called 'Britain Today'. Your class teacher could select small numbers of you in turn to leave the display and look at what the others are doing. What themes seem to be most strongly represented? Is this a reflection of life in your area or of how you perceive life in Britain today generally?

VINEGAR TOM

by Caryl Churchill

CAST (in order of appearance)

BELLRINGER
MARGERY
JACK
PACKER
GOODY
JOAN
SUSAN
ALICE
BETTY
ELLEN

10 speaking parts. Doubling possible.

On the surface one might say that *Vinegar Tom* was a play about witches. A closer look might suggest that it's about how women are accused of being witches. Go deeper again and one might see that the play also makes statements about *why* women are accused of being witches. In many ways *Vinegar Tom* is a historical play, inspired by the many accounts of the witch-hunts of the seventeenth century. In the turmoil just after the Civil War, new ways of thinking were struggling for general acceptance. The Parliamentarians (Roundheads) tended to apply the teachings of the Bible in strict and very male-orientated ways. Caryl Churchill's play takes place in a world in which the puritanical Roundheads are trying to create a more modern and 'professional' society. The old-fashioned practices of 'cunning women' with their folk medicine and herbal remedies were seen as a threat to progress. Caryl Churchill notes that 'the women accused of witchcraft were often those on the edges of society: old, poor, single, sexually unconventional.' The qualities of such women – notably their skill with herbs, their knowledge of human nature and ability to give good advice – had been valued in their own communities. But then, as always, unconventional people were seen as a threat by those in authority.

Accusing a woman of being a witch was a way of punishing her for not being 'normal', and also a warning to other women to fall into line or suffer the consequences.

Caryl Churchill has written a play not so much about witchcraft as about how women saw themselves and how changes in society affected that. There is a clear and strong undercurrent in the play suggesting that society today is still in the grip of many of the attitudes of that time. The story follows the fortunes of Alice and her mother Joan. Alice is pursued by a frustrated married man, Jack. When she refuses to go to bed with him he calls her a witch. In the mean time his equally bitter wife, Margery, takes out her frustration on Joan by accusing her also of being a witch. The arrival of a witchfinder and his assistant in the village gives those who want it the chance to 'get even' and settle their petty grievances in a gruesome way.

The style of the play

Vinegar Tom is a blunt and cold play. The audience are shown scenes depicting how the witch-hunt affects the local people. The story of Alice and Joan is told in a straightforward, chronological way. The play is interspersed with songs which seem to relate the events of 300 years ago to the present day.

The extract

Jack and his wife Margery both have personal reasons for wanting vengeance on Alice and Joan. Alice's friend Susan has just lost a baby and needs to blame someone. A local cunning woman, Ellen, is another easy target for the Witchfinder, Packer, and his sadistic assistant, Goody Haskins, who have just arrived in the village. The other characters in the extract are Betty – another friend of Alice's – and a Bellringer who announces the arrival of the Witchfinder.

Scene fourteen

BELLRINGER   Whereas if anyone has any complaint against any woman for a witch, let them go to the townhall and lay their complaint. For a man is in town that is a famous finder of witches and has had above thirty hanged in the country round and he will discover if they are or no. Whereas if   5
anyone has any complaint against any woman for a witch, let them go . . .

MARGERY   Stopped the butter.

JACK   Killed the calves.

MARGERY   Struck me in the head.   10

JACK   Lamed my hand.

MARGERY   Struck me in the stomach.

JACK   Bewitched my organ.

MARGERY   When I boiled my urine she came.

JACK   Blooded her and made my hand well.   15

MARGERY   Burnt her thatch.

JACK   And Susan, her friend, is like possessed screaming and crying and lay two days without speaking.

MARGERY   Susan's baby turned blue and its limbs twisted and it died.   20

JACK   Boy threw stones and called them witch, and after he vomited pins and straw.

MARGERY   Big nasty cat she has in her bed and sends it to people's dairies.

JACK   A rat's her imp.   25

MARGERY   And the great storm last night brought a tree down in the lane, who made that out of a clear sky?

PACKER   I thank God that he has brought me again where I am needed. Don't be afraid any more. You have been in great danger but the devil can never overcome the faithful. For   30
God in his mercy has called me and shown me a wonderful way of finding out witches, which is finding the place on the body of the witch made insensitive to pain by the devil. So that if you prick that place with a pin no blood comes out and the witch feels nothing at all.   35

PACKER *and* GOODY *take* JOAN, *and* GOODY *holds her, while* PACKER *pulls up her skirts and pricks her legs.* JOAN *curses and screams throughout.* PACKER *and* GOODY *abuse her: a short sharp moment of great noise and confusion.*

GOODY   Hold still you old witch. Devil not help you now, no good calling him. Strong for your age, that's the devil's strength in her, see. Hold still, you stinking old strumpet . . .

PACKER   Hold your noise, witch, how can we tell what we're doing? Ah, ah, there's for you devil, there's blood, and there's blood, where's your spot, we'll find you out Satan . . . 40

JOAN   Damn you to hell, oh Christ help me! Ah, ah, you're hurting, let go, damn you, oh sweet God, oh you devils, oh devil take you . . . 45

PACKER   There, there, no blood here, Goody Haskins. Here's her spot. Hardly a speck here.

GOODY   How she cries the old liar, pretending it hurts her.

PACKER   There's one for hanging, stand aside there. We've others to attend to. Next please, Goody. 50

GOODY *takes* ALICE. PACKER *helps, and her skirts are thrown over her head while he pricks her. She tries not to cry out.*

GOODY   Why so much blood?

PACKER   The devil's cunning here.

GOODY   She's not crying much, she can't feel it.

PACKER   Have I the spot though? Which is the spot? There. There. There. No, I haven't the spot. Oh, it's tiring work. 55 Set this one aside. Maybe there's others will speak against her and let us know more clearly what she is.

ALICE *is stood aside.*

PACKER   If anyone here knows anything more of this woman why she might be a witch, I charge them in God's name to speak out, or the guilt of filthy witchcraft will be on you for 60 concealing it.

SUSAN   I know something of her.

PACKER   Don't be shy then girl, speak out.

ALICE   Susan, what you doing? Don't speak against me.

SUSAN   Don't let her at me.   65

ALICE   You'll have me hanged.

SUSAN *starts to shriek hysterically.*

GOODY   Look, she's bewitched.

MARGERY   It's Alice did it to her.

ALICE   Susan, stop.

SUSAN   Alice. Alice. Alice.   70

PACKER   Take the witch out and the girl may be quiet.

GOODY *takes* ALICE *off.* SUSAN *stops.*

MARGERY   See that.

JACK   Praise God I escaped such danger.

SUSAN   She met with the devil, she told me, like a man in black
she met him in the night and did uncleanness with him, and   75
ever after she was not herself but wanted to be with the
devil again. She took me to a cunning woman and they
made me take a foul potion to destroy the baby in my womb
and it was destroyed. And the cunning woman said she
would teach Alice her wicked magic, and she'd have powers   80
and not everyone could learn that, but Alice could because
she's a witch, and the cunning woman gave her something
to call the devil, and she tried to call him, and she made a
puppet, and stuck pins in, and tried to make me believe that
was the devil, but that was my baby girl, and next day she   85
was sick and her face blue and limbs all twisted up and she
died. And I don't want to see her.

PACKER   These cunning women are worst of all. Everyone
hates witches who do harm but good witches they go to for
help and come into the devil's power without knowing it.   90
The infection will spread through the whole country if we
don't stop it. Yes, all witches deserve death, and the good
witch even more than the bad one. Oh God, do not let your
kingdom be overrun by the devil. And you, girl, you went to
this good witch, and you destroyed the child in your womb   95
by witchcraft, which is a grievous offence. And you were
there when this puppet was stuck with pins, and consented
to the death of your own baby daughter?

SUSAN   No, I didn't. I didn't consent. I never wished her harm.
Oh if I was angry sometimes or cursed her for crying, I   100
never meant it. I'd take it back if I could have her back. I
never meant to harm her.

PACKER   You can't take your curses back, you cursed her to
death. That's two of your children you killed. And what
other harm have you done? Don't look amazed, you'll speak   105
soon enough. We'll prick you as you pricked your babies.

Scene fifteen

GOODY *takes* SUSAN *and* PACKER *pulls up her skirt.*

GOODY   There's no man finds more witches than Henry
Packer. He can tell by their look, he says, but of course he
has more ways than that. He's read all the books and he's
travelled. He says the reason there's so much witchcraft in   110
England is England is too soft with its witches, for in Europe
and Scotland they are hanged and burned and if they are not
penitent they are burnt alive, but in England they are only
hanged. And the ways of discovering witches are not so
good here, for in other countries they have thrumbscrews   115
and racks and the bootikens which is said to be the worst
pain in the world, for it fits tight over the legs from ankle to
knee and is driven tighter and tighter till the legs are crushed
as small as might be and the blood and marrow spout out
and the bones crushed and the legs made unserviceable   120
forever. And very few continue their lies and denials then. In
England we haven't got such thorough ways, our ways are
slower but they get the truth in the end when a fine skilful
man like Henry Packer is onto them. He's well worth the
twenty shillings a time, and I get the same, which is very   125
good of him to insist on and well worth it though some folk
complain and say, 'what, the price of a cow, just to have a
witch hanged?' But I say to them think of the expense a
witch is to you in the damage she does to property, such as a
cow killed one or two pounds, a horse maybe four pounds,   130
besides all the pigs and sheep at a few shiillings a time, and

chickens at sixpence all adds up. For two pounds and our expenses at the inn, you have all that saving, besides knowing you're free of the threat of sudden illness and death. Yes, it's interesting work being a searcher and nice to 135 do good at the same time as earning a living. Better than staying home a widow. I'd end up like the old women you see, soft in the head and full of spite with their muttering and spells. I keep healthy keeping the country healthy. It's an honour to work with a great professional. 140

Scene sixteen

BETTY I'm frightened to come any more. They'll say I'm a witch.

ELLEN Are they saying I'm a witch?

BETTY They say because I screamed that was the devil in me. And when I ran out of the house they say where was I going 145 if not to meet other witches. And some know I come to see you.

ELLEN Nobody's said it yet to my face.

BETTY But the doctor says he'll save me. He says I'm not a witch, he says I'm ill. He says I'm his patient so I can't be a 150 witch. He says he's making me better. I hope I can be better.

ELLEN You get married, Betty, that's safest.

BETTY But I want to be left alone. You know I do.

ELLEN Left alone for what? To be like me? There's no doctor going to save me from being called a witch. Your best 155 chance of being left alone is marry a rich man, because it's part of his honour to have a wife who does nothing. He has his big house and rose garden and trout stream, he just needs a fine lady to make it complete and you can be that. You can sing and sit on the lawn and change your dresses 160 and order the dinner. That's the best you can do. What would you rather? Marry a poor man and work all day? Or go on as you're going, go on strange? That's not safe. Plenty of girls feel like you've been feeling, just for a bit. But you're not one to go on with it. 165

BETTY If it's true there's witches, maybe I've been bewitched.
If the witches are stopped maybe I'll get well.
ELLEN You'll get well, my dear, and you'll get married, and
you'll tell your children about the witches.
BETTY What's going to happen? Will you be all right? 170
ELLEN You go home now. You don't want them finding you
here.

  BETTY *goes*.

I could ask to be swum. They think the water won't keep a
witch in, for Christ's baptism sake, so if a woman floats
she's a witch. And if she sinks they have to let her go. I 175
could sink. Any fool can sink. It's how to sink without
drowning. It's whether they get you out. No, why should I
ask to be half drowned? I've done nothing. I'll explain to
them what I do. It's healing, not harm. There's no devil in it.
If I keep calm and explain it, they can't hurt me. 180

If you float

If you float you're a witch
If you scream you're a witch
If you sink, then you're dead anyway.
If you cure you're a witch
Or impure you're a witch 185
Whatever you do, you must pay.
Fingers are pointed, a knock at the door,
You may be a mother, a child or a whore.
If you complain you're a witch
Or you're lame you're a witch 190
Any marks or deviations count for more.
Got big tits you're a witch
Fall to bits you're a witch
He likes them young, concupiscent and poor.
Fingers are pointed, a knock on the door, 195
They're coming to get you, do you know what for?
So don't drop a stitch

My poor little bitch
If you're making a spell
Do it well. 200
Deny it you're bad
Admit it you're mad
Say nothing at all
They'll damn you to hell.

Understanding the text

1 Read through the script and make a note, as you do so, of all the comments or remarks that might be used as evidence that someone is a witch. Look carefully at your list and divide them into two sets: those that appear to be based on fact, and those that seem to be based on superstition.

2 List the various methods of discovering witches mentioned in the extract. What do you think the author's intention is in including these descriptions?

3 What reasons does Goody Haskins give for working for Packer? Consider her comment: 'Better than staying at home a widow. I'd end up like the old women you see, soft in the head and full of spite with their muttering and spells' (lines 136–9). In what way does this affect your opinion of her and what she is doing?

4 Why do you think Ellen, the local 'cunning woman', says, 'There's no doctor going to save me from being called a witch'? Why do you think getting married will help save Betty from being accused?

5 Scene 14 seems to consist of a number of different sections, as if time has been condensed and the audience are only being shown the 'edited highlights' of the events rather than one whole scene that actually took place. Make a note of where each block of time seems to end and a new one begins.

Producing the scene

1 No stage directions are given as to where each scene might be taking place. Suggest:
- a possible setting for each scene
- a way of representing that place simply
- an appropriate lighting state for each scene.

2 With so many quick changes of scene it might be easier to act the play on a very bare stage. List three advantages and three possible disadvantages of this method.

3 In the opening section of this extract where Jack and Margery are giving details of what they think Joan has done to them the lines are very short, blunt and quite rhythmical. Try to rehearse lines 8–16 emphasising a rhythm. In groups of four or five make up a few more accusations in the same style and experiment with ways of speaking them to a set beat. Try whispering them and see if this might also create a good effect.

4 Make a set of 'director's notes' which could be used to advise the actress playing Goody Haskins when she is tackling her long speech (lines 107–40). Make a note of anything that she ought to do, or anything that is going on in the background. Remember, any action should add to rather than distract from what she is saying.

5 An alternative to singing 'If You Float' would be to use 'choral speech'. In groups of at least four divide the lines up between different speakers, for example:

1 If you float you're a witch
2 If you scream you're a witch
3 If you sink
4 then you're dead anyway.

and so on. Some lines could be said by two or more people together and some perhaps by the whole group. The point is to capture the rhythm of the writing whilst emphasising the point it is trying to make.

6 Consider the way you have decided to deliver the lines of 'If You Float' and now consider how you might position or move the chorus around to make a visual as well as an aural impact on an audience.

Further development

1 Packer seems to have already decided who is guilty. Improvise a scene in which one person is trying to defend herself against one or more others who have already decided on her guilt.

2 In the extract Alice is betrayed by her friend Susan, who then tries to deny that she meant what she said. Imagine a scene in which the two characters meet again in a cell. How would Susan explain her action and what would Alice's reaction be?

3 What sort of circumstances might lead someone to betray a close friend? Make up a story in which someone comes under pressure in some way which results in a betrayal. You might be able to think of actual historical events where you can imagine this happening.

4 This extract presents a number of assumptions about women who behave in ways which don't fit in with society's expectations. Is there anything that girls do today which causes people to assume something about them? What sort of assumptions, for example, would a girl who wanted to be a lorry driver have to face up to? Write or improvise a scene in which a woman has to face up to such assumptions. (If you are interested in this area you may enjoy Clare Luckham's play *Trafford Tanzi*.)

5 Imagine that the tide of history turned in such a way as to place women in positions of power whilst Packer was still alive. Set up a courtroom scene in which Packer is tried for crimes against women. What assumptions might be made about the type of man he is and why he was doing what he was doing? Who would give evidence against him and how could he be defended?

6 Actually staging an execution could create a number of problems. It would be important not to do it in such a way that the audience either laughed or felt sick – this would take their attention away from the unfairness of what was being done. Experiment with ways of staging such a scene which would successfully make the audience feel anger at the injustice.

7 Think of a group of people from any period of history (including the present day), who are seen as easy targets for persecution in the same way as women are in *Vinegar Tom*. Look carefully at the language of 'If You Float' and use the style as the basis for a piece of choral speech of your own which explores the unfairness of how certain groups of people are treated.

THE COUNTRY WIFE
by *William Wycherley*

CAST (in order of appearance)

SIR JASPER FIDGET
LADY FIDGET
HORNER
QUACK
MRS SQUEAMISH
OLD LADY SQUEAMISH

6 speaking parts. No doubling.

When the English Civil War broke out in 1642 all of the theatres in London were closed down. For the next 18 years the country lived under the austere rule of Cromwell's Parliamentarians with their strict moralistic attitudes. When Charles II was restored to the throne in 1660 many people sighed with relief and looked forward to having some fun again. The period that followed is called 'The Restoration', and it was during this time that some of the cleverest and most finely crafted comedies in the English language were written. Many of them were very bawdy and suggest that after the soberness of Cromwell's rule, society went the other way and took on a devil-may-care attitude.

The Country Wife is in many ways a typical comedy of the period in that it has a complex plot and a largish cast of comic characters, all of whom seem to represent a particular human failing. Although the play is a comedy, one can see that the author is being critical of the immorality in society – it's hard really to sympathise with any of the characters.

The basic story is as follows: Horner, a notorious lady-killer, returns from France and has a doctor spread the rumour that he is impotent and his lady-killing days are over. Horner's male friends think it is highly amusing that he is now impotent, and start to taunt him by leaving him alone with their wives – something they would never have done before! Of course, this is the aim of Horner's cunning plan. Once alone with the ladies he tells them of his deception and, safe in the knowledge that their husbands think Horner is no threat, they start to have some fun.

The jokes in the play rely mainly on 'double entendre' or double meanings. For all its bawdiness the play is making a critical comment on a society that was so hell bent on having fun that it had stopped caring for people. The husbands use their wives to tease Horner, and so when they are cuckolded they are really getting their just deserts. The women in the play are portrayed as being greedy and unfeeling and so when at the end they are forced to accept their unsatisfactory marriages, we can't really feel much sympathy for them. Only the roguish Horner seems in a good humour at the end, which might suggest that in a society based on greed and hypocrisy only the utterly heartless can win.

The style of the play

As is usual with plays of this period, *The Country Wife* is rather longer than most modern plays. However, the dialogue is full of wit and with many of the jokes referring to contemporary trends and events one can see why they were so popular at the time. The language is a little more difficult for us now, but the overall style is similar to modern farces and situation comedies, with much of the humour deriving from hectic action, pretence and misunderstanding. The staging of plays at this time was elaborate, with highly decorated three-dimensional scenery and ornate costumes. Women were accepted on stage for the first time and the whole business of going to the theatre was an important social event for anyone who wanted to be noticed in polite society.

The extract

This is a famous comic scene and shows what a master of double-entendre Wycherley was. Lady Fidget has told her husband that she is going to buy some china, but really she is about to have an encounter with Horner. Unluckily, Sir Jasper, her husband, also turns up at Horner's house. With some quick thinking, though, the lovers pull the wool over his eyes and disappear into the next room, leaving the foolishly trusting husband laughing at what he believes to be Horner's inability to do anything with his wife. Into this scene comes Mrs Squeamish who also wants the company of Horner. The conversation that follows clearly means different things to the different characters . . .

Enter SIR JASPER FIDGET.

SIR JASPER How now!

LADY FIDGET [*aside*] O my husband – prevented – and what's
almost as bad, found with my arms about another man –
that will appear too much – what shall I say? – Sir Jasper
come hither. I am trying if Mr Horner were ticklish, and   5
he's as ticklish as can be. I love to torment the confounded
toad; let you and I tickle him.

SIR JASPER No, your ladyship will tickle him better without
me, I suppose. But is this your buying china? I thought you
had been at the china house.   10

HORNER [*aside*] China house, that's my cue, I must take it. –
A pox! Can't you keep your impertinent wives at home?
Some men are troubled with the husbands, but I with the
wives. But I'd have you to know, since I cannot be your
journeyman by night, I will not be your drudge by day, to   15
squire your wife about and be your man of straw, or
scarecrow, only to pies and jays that would be nibbling at
your forbidden fruit. I shall be shortly the hackney
gentleman-usher of the town.

SIR JASPER [*aside*] Heh, heh, he! Poor fellow, he's in the right   20
on't, faith. To squire women about for other folks is as
ungrateful an employment as to tell money for other folks. –
Heh, he, he! Ben't angry, Horner.

LADY FIDGET No, 'tis I have more reason to be angry, who am
left by you, to go abroad indecently alone; or, what is more   25
indecent, to pin myself upon such ill-bred people of your
acquaintance as this is.

SIR JASPER Nay, prithee, what has he done?

LADY FIDGET Nay, he has done nothing.

SIR JASPER But what d'ye take ill, if he has done nothing?   30

LADY FIDGET Hah, hah, hah! Faith, I can't but laugh however.
Why d'ye think the unmannerly toad would not come down
to me to the coach? I was fain to come up to fetch him, or
go without him, which I was resolved not to do; for he
knows china very well, and has himself very good, but will   35

line 17   *pies and jays*   foolish men
line 18–19   *hackney gentleman-usher*   hired servant

not let me see it lest I should beg some. But I will find it out, and have what I came for yet.

Exit LADY FIDGET, *and locks the door, followed by* HORNER *to the door.*

HORNER [*apart to* LADY FIDGET] Lock the door, madam. [*Aloud*] So, she has got into my chamber, and locked me out. Oh, the impertinency of woman-kind! Well, Sir Jasper,   40
plain dealing is a jewel; if ever you suffer your wife to trouble me again here, she shall carry you home a pair of horns, by my Lord Mayor she shall; though I cannot furnish you myself, you are sure, yet I'll find a way.

SIR JASPER [*aside*] Hah, ha, he! At my first coming in, and   45
finding her arms about him, tickling him it seems, I was half jealous, but now I see my folly. – Heh, he, he! Poor Horner.

HORNER Nay, though you laugh now, 'twill be my turn ere long. Oh women, more impertinent, more cunning, and more mischievous than their monkeys, and to me almost as   50
ugly! Now is she throwing my things about, and rifling all I have, but I'll get into her the back way, and so rifle her for it –

SIR JASPER Hah, ha, ha! Poor angry Horner.

HORNER Stay here a little, I'll ferret her out to you presently, I   55
warrant.

Exit HORNER *at the other door.*

SIR JASPER [SIR JASPER *calls through the door to his wife, she answers from within*] Wife! My Lady Fidget! Wife! He is coming into you the back way.

LADY FIDGET Let him come, and welcome, which way he will.   60

SIR JASPER He'll catch you, and use you roughly, and be too strong for you.

LADY FIDGET Don't you trouble yourself, let him if he can.

QUACK [*behind*] This indeed, I could not have believed from him, nor any but my own eyes.   65

Enter MRS SQUEAMISH.

MRS SQUEAMISH Where's this woman-hater, this toad, this ugly, greasy, dirty sloven?

SIR JASPER [*aside*]   So, the women all will have him ugly. Methinks he is a comely person, but his wants make his form contemptible to 'em. And 'tis e'en as my wife said   70
yesterday, talking of him, that a proper handsome eunuch was as ridiculous a thing as a gigantic coward.

MRS SQUEAMISH   Sir Jasper, your servant. Where is the odious beast?

SIR JASPER   He's within in his chamber, with my wife. She's   75
playing the wag with him.

MRS SQUEAMISH   Is she so? And he's a clownish beast, he'll give her no quarter, he'll play the wag with her again, let me tell you. Come, let's go help her. – What, the door's locked?

SIR JASPER   Ay, my wife locked it –   80

MRS SQUEAMISH   Did she so? Let us break it open then.

SIR JASPER   No, no, he'll do her no hurt.

MRS SQUEAMISH   No. – [*Aside*] But is there no other way to get into 'em? Whither goes this? I will disturb 'em.

Exit MRS SQUEAMISH *at another door.*
Enter OLD LADY SQUEAMISH.

OLD LADY SQUEAMISH   Where is this harlotry, this impudent   85
baggage, this rambling tomrigg? O Sir Jasper, I'm glad to see you here. Did you not see my vile grandchild come in hither just now?

SIR JASPER   Yes.

OLD LADY SQUEAMISH   Ay, but where is she then? Where is she?   90
Lord, Sir Jasper, I have e'en rattled myself to pieces in pursuit of her. But can you tell what she makes here? They say below, no woman lodges here.

SIR JASPER   No.

OLD LADY SQUEAMISH   No! What does she here then? Say, if it   95
be not a woman's lodging, what makes she here? But are you sure no woman lodges here?

SIR JASPER   No, nor no man neither. This is Mr Horner's lodging.

OLD LADY SQUEAMISH   Is it so? Are you sure?   100

SIR JASPER   Yes, yes.

line 86   *tomrigg*   tomboy

107

OLD LADY SQUEAMISH   So; then there's no hurt in't, I hope. But where is he?

SIR JASPER   He's in the next room with my wife.

OLD LADY SQUEAMISH   Nay, if you trust him with your wife, I   105
may with my Biddy. They say he's a merry harmless man now, e'en as harmless a man as ever came out of Italy with a good voice, and as pretty harmless company for a lady, as a snake without his teeth.

SIR JASPER   Ay, ay, poor man.   110

Enter MRS SQUEAMISH.

MRS SQUEAMISH   I can't find 'em. – Oh, are you here grandmother? I followed, you must know, My Lady Fidget hither; 'tis the prettiest lodging, and I have been staring on the prettiest pictures.

Enter LADY FIDGET *with a piece of china in her hand, and* HORNER *following.*

LADY FIDGET   And I have been toiling and moiling for the   115
prettiest piece of china, my dear.

HORNER   Nay, she has been too hard for me, do what I could.

MRS SQUEAMISH   O Lord, I'll have some china too, good Mr Horner. Don't think to give other people china, and me none. Come in with me too.   120

HORNER   Upon my honour, I have none left now.

MRS SQUEAMISH   Nay, nay, I have known you deny your china before now, but you shan't put me off so. Come –

HORNER   This lady had the last there.

LADY FIDGET   Yes indeed, madam, to my certain knowledge he   125
has no more left.

MRS SQUEAMISH   Oh, but it may be he may have some you could not find.

LADY FIDGET   What? D'ye think if he had had any left, I would not have had it too? For we women of quality never think   130
we have china enough.

HORNER   Do not take it ill, I cannot make china for you all, but I will have a roll-wagon for you too another time.

line 115   *toiling and moiling*   working hard
line 133   *roll wagon*   vehicle for carrying goods

MRS SQUEAMISH Thank you, dear toad.

LADY FIDGET [to HORNER, *aside*] What do you mean by that 135
promise?

HORNER [*apart to* LADY FIDGET] Alas, she has an innocent,
literal understanding.

OLD LADY SQUEAMISH Poor Mr Horner, he has enough to do to
please you all, I see. 140

HORNER Ay, madam, you see how they use me.

OLD LADY SQUEAMISH Poor gentleman, I pity you.

HORNER I thank you madam, I could never find pity, but from
such reverend ladies as you are; the young ones will never
spare a man. 145

MRS SQUEAMISH Come come, beast, and go dine with us, for
we shall want a man at hombre after dinner.

HORNER That's all their use of me madam, you see.

---

line 147   *hombre*   a card game

Understanding the text

1 The 'aside' was a common feature in plays of this time. Look at the number of times it is used in this scene and suggest at least two ways in which it helps the audience appreciate the scene more.

2 Another feature of plays of this period was the use of names that say something about the characters who own them. Write down the names of the characters in this scene and suggest what sort of people they might be.

3 Do you think Mrs Squeamish knows what is going on behind the locked door? Find at least two comments that suggest she does.

4 The characters in the scene are quite rude both to and about each other. Pick out three lines which suggest that they tend to see people as animals rather than humans.

Producing the scene

1 Draw a plan view of a possible set for this scene. In addition to marking where the doors are you will need to consider how the characters can come in and out without bumping into each other, so note down which doors should be used for the various entrances and exits in the scene. Mark out your set on the floor if possible and walk through your suggested entrances and exits to see if they work.

2 Design a costume for one of the characters which, like his/her name, reflects his/her character.

3 Look at Lady Fidget's first speech.

- To whom is the aside addressed and at which point does it change to becoming her own ordinary speech again?
- How can the actress playing this part make the two parts of the speech different so as not to confuse the audience?
- Look at the other side and decide what advice you would give the actors who have to say them.

4 Pick out as many instances as you can in the scene where what someone says may be different from what they actually mean. Lines 115–33 contain probably the best examples of this. Explain how the actors could deliver these lines to achieve the best comic effect.

5 How would you position the actors on the stage at the end of this scene in order to show the audience

- who knows what is going on
- who thinks that they know what is going on
- who hasn't a clue?

One way of doing this would be to form a tableau in groups and then have each character speek aloud her thoughts about the others on stage. By doing this you may be able to suggest to each other slight adjustments in their position and expression.

6 Unknown to the visitors, Horner's doctor – Quack – is watching this whole scene in order to see how well the plan is working. Draw a picture or diagram showing how he might be concealed on the stage, but still able to make his aside without being obvious to the other characters in the room.

Further development

1 Get into small groups. Each member of the group invents a name which suggests a particular type of character and writes it on a piece of paper. The papers are folded and put in the middle and everyone takes one. Quickly decide on a place where these people might meet and improvise a conversation in which the character types begin to show themselves.

2 Two people are standing talking about something. (It could be *anything*.) Two others arrive, listen, and then join in the conversation. But because what the first two are saying is *ambiguous* (could have more than one meaning, like much of the language in *The Country Wife*), the other two get completely the wrong idea about this conversation. The comedy in

the improvisation should arise, as in *The Country Wife*, from the fact that whilst they are all involved in the same conversation the meaning is very different for each of them.

3 A classic scene in farce is where a husband or wife is found being unfaithful but manages, somehow, to give a perfectly plausible reason for what he/she is doing. Can you think of any times when you, or anyone you know, have successfully talked your way out of a tight spot. In pairs number yourselves 1 and 2. Number 1 freezes in a position where she has clearly been 'caught in the act'. Number 2 opens the improvisation with the line 'What are you doing?' From here on number 2 asks questions which number 1 has to answer as plausibly as possible. See how long you can keep this going.

4 Make up a scene in which someone has the wool pulled over her eyes because she is too stupid or too self-confident to see what is really going on.

5 Although this is both a funny scene and, indeed, a funny play, it is making some serious criticisms of the society of the time. List any TV shows, films or plays that seem to you to make serious points through comedy. Pick a subject that you feel strongly about and see if you can adopt some of the same techniques in an improvisation.

THE GOLDEN PATHWAY ANNUAL

by *John Harding and John Burrows*

CAST (in order of appearance)

MADEMOISELLE
MICHAEL
THE HEAD

3 speaking parts. No doubling.

If you've come across the term 'baby boom' elsewhere you will know that it refers to the period of fifteen years or so after World War 2 in which the population increased dramatically. There are many different reasons for this sudden growth. Perhaps people thought that the world after the war would be a bright, hopeful place to live in. There was a growing prosperity and the Government strongly urged that a new Britain should rise from the ruins of the old. The 1944 Education Act had improved everyone's chances of getting a decent secondary education and soon colleges and polytechnics were offering Higher Education to many who, before the War, would have had only a very slim chance of studying at that level. New technology was rapidly changing the world. The race to get man into space started and with more and more homes acquiring television sets, people became more aware and better informed of what was going on in the world. By the end of the 1950s many people must have been able to see the possibility of an exciting and prosperous future. The 1960s brought all manner of new ideas in art, theatre and education, and technology seemed to develop at an even faster pace.

However, by the end of the 1960s the dream seemed to be fading. There was, for example, widespread rioting in 1968 with students protesting against American involvement in Vietnam. Many thought that although technology was progressing, society was not. Civil Rights movements in both the US and Northern Ireland ended in bloodshed as the protesters challenged the authority of the state. Whereas at the beginning of the decade prospects for employment had been excellent, by the end of it more and more workers were being laid off. Machines were more efficient and more economical; some people began to find that despite their education there was no job waiting for them.

The Golden Pathway Annual traces the story of one boy, Michael Peters, through these years, from the return of his father after the War with 'a lovely twinkle' in his eye, up to 1968 when the only job he can get involves sacking his own father.

The style of the play

Overall the play could be described as a comedy; it certainly seems to make audiences laugh a lot — older people because they are reminded both of the traumas of growing up and the events of the period, and younger ones because they can see Michael having the same trouble with his parents as they are with theirs! The writing is quite straightforward. The play is divided into a series of short scenes depicting key moments in Michael's life. The stage directions suggest that it is played on a conventional proscenium arch stage. Only two chairs and a few props are needed, but an important part of the set is the backdrop which should be a huge Start-Rite Shoes advertisement. The advert shows two young children setting off along a golden road and the slogan below reads: 'Children's shoes have far to go, Start-Rite and they'll walk happily ever after'. As well as being a very nostalgic symbol, the picture represents Michael's story in a sad way; he does 'Start-Rite' but things don't turn out as either he or his parents thought they would.

The extract

As a bright boy Michael would have gone to a grammar school. However, like many adolescents, he is much more interested in his French teacher and the exploits of James Bond (or whoever the current media hero is) than in learning French. In this scene he slips into his own fantasy world. Notice how the writers achieve a great deal of comedy through the unlikely mix of the world of James Bond with Michael's real situation.

Scene 5

1963 Michael Peters, seeing himself as James Bond, takes on 'The Head' and gives the French Assistante more than she bargained for.

    Enter MADEMOISELLE *and* MICHAEL.

MLLE   Bonjour, Michel. Comment ça va?

MICHAEL   Assez bien, merci, Mademoiselle Leblanc. Et vous?

MLLE   Comme ci, comme ça. Vous êtes seul aujourd'hui?

MICHAEL   Oui. Je cris que les autres sont absents.

MLLE   Eh, bien, la conversation française entre nous deux. 5
Qu'est-ce que vous avez fait cette semaine?

MICHAEL   Presque rien, comme d'habitude: les leçons, les devoirs, rien de plus.

MLLE   Mais pensez. Nous devons parler. Qu'est ce que vous pensez des lycéens anglais comme vous? 10

MICHAEL   Er, er, je crois que, je ne suis pas certain de—répétez vous, s'il vous plaît.

MLLE   Oh Peters! Every week we go through this charade of French conversation. You always tell me you have done nothing, you are just a schoolboy, so we talk of autumn, 15 pieces of theatre, la vie française. [*Fantasy begins and* MICHAEL *becomes James Bond for the rest of scene.*] Let us be frank. You are not Michael Peters, and I am not Françoise Leblanc. We both know why we are here, and time is getting short. You can trust me, James Bond, 007 of 20 Her Majesty's Secret Service!

MICHAEL   Incroyable! What makes you think I am not Michael Peters?

MLLE   One or two little things I have noticed. First, there is your physique: superb. Second, under that ridiculous 25 English schoolboy blazer you wear a handmade sea island cotton shirt with your black silk knitted tie. Then you do not take school dinners.

MICHAEL   Many of the boys bring a packed lunch.

MLLE   Underdone tournedos à la sauce Béarnaise with coeur 30 d'artichaut and a bottle of Tattainger Blanc de Brut '43?

MICHAEL   So I like good food and drink.

MLLE   You overtook the 183 bus this morning on your way to
school in a 1930 4½-litre supercharged Bentley.

MICHAEL   I thought the L plates would fool you.   35

MLLE   You were wearing your Arnold Riley cap, Bond.

MICHAEL   What are you going to do then, keep me in after
school?

MLLE   Don't think it hasn't crossed my mind, James. I am
your French contact, Ophelia Plenty.   40

MICHAEL   All in good time. [*aside*] Something about the jutting
swell of her pointed hillocks, her square-toed shoes, and the
thick weight of hair at the nape of the neck told me she was
no ordinary French Assistante. How did you get into the
Service?   45

MLLE   My father was a great chef, pressed into service by the
Nazis during the occupation, but he passed on information
to the Resistance. When the Gestapo shot him, my mother,
my brothers and sisters, I alone escaped, and vowed to fight
always for freedom.   50

MICHAEL   Good girl. Did your father serve rognon de veau
with pommes sautés followed by fraises des bois?

MLLE   Of course. Oh James, it has been an agony, waiting till
I could reveal myself. I want you, James. I want you to do
everything to me. Everything you've ever done to a woman.   55
Now, please.

MICHAEL   Certainly, choux-fleure. What have you been able to
find out?

MLLE   Someone in the school is attempting to brainwash the
sixth form.   60

MICHAEL   Right. The boys have been implanted with something which makes them completely servile. It's pathetic:
instead of living the life of red-blooded young males, they
stay in at night doing homework, they do virtually without
money and sex, display amazing anxiety over exams, and   65
are prepared to bully younger boys of their own class in an
obsequious desire to please masters. But who is behind it
all?

MLLE   One of the arch fiends of all time. He's subtle, ruthless,
mad, and physically revolting. So important is he in the   70
underworld, they call him The Head.

MICHAEL   The Head! Of course, his earlobes are too long, and his fat lips always wet. But what is his aim?

MLLE   He wants to rule the world through these automatons, and he holds sway over them with a terrible promise: success. Success that is always just another exam away. Careful, James. The skeleton butt of your .25 Beretta is interfering with the mysterious promise of my folded thighs.   75

MICHAEL   We must liquidate him.

MLLE   You do it James. I can watch. When this is all over, we could get married. You do love me just a little, don't you, James?   80

MICHAEL   Thanks for telling me what you know, Miss Plentsky.

MLLE   James!   85

MICHAEL   You bitch! You're a double agent. You're SMERSH.

MLLE   Oh, James, I feel so guilty. How did you know?

MICHAEL   Rognon de veau is served with pommes soufflés, not sautés.

MLLE   But they forced me, James. I love you.   90

MICHAEL   You would have used me to get rid of The Head, then killed me and used his secrets to control innocent schoolboys in Georgia for your own vile communistic ends!

MLLE   Oh, it's true! It's true!

Enter THE HEAD. *He holds a cane.*

THE HEAD   I congratulate you, Mr Bond. A remarkable piece   95
of deduction. Such a pity it should come to nothing.

MLLE
MICHAEL   } The Head!

THE HEAD   I have heard everything, my dear boy. How clever of my old school chum M to infiltrate 007 as a schoolboy. But for Ophelia Plentsky, your cover would remain intact,   100
so I think it only fair that she should die first and leave us boys together, don't you? [*He stabs her with the end of the cane. She dies slowly.*]

MICHAEL   You swine!

THE HEAD   Come, Mr Bond, she is our mutual enemy.   105

MICHAEL   But she is a beautiful woman!

THE HEAD How touching and quaint that you should fall victim to the weakness of flesh we call lust. You should know never to trust a woman, James. Now she's quiet, we can enjoy ourelves. No heroics please. [*He rips open* 110 *Michael's shirt, draws blood with cane.*] What fine red blood you have, James. You will write me a thousand lines in it before you die.

MICHEAL You're mad, The Head!

THE HEAD Tush, I think 'I must not be a secret agent in class' 115 would be appropriate, don't you?

MICHAEL What do you hope to gain with this scheme of yours?

THE HEAD Do not play the dull and stupid schoolboy, James. You know you are capable of much better work. I already 120 control the most intelligent young men in England. What is to stop me taking over the world?

MICHAEL Damn the Welfare State!

THE HEAD Quite. I think perhaps I should cane you to death, no? Drop your trousers. Bend over. [*He is paralysed as he* 125 *draws his arm back*.] Aagh! But what is happening to me?

MICHAEL You underestimated me, The Head. As I dropped my trousers, I released a tiny spider stolen from the biology lab. It has bitten your jugular.

THE HEAD Poisonous insects in the school? The P.T.A. 130 wouldn't allow it!

MICHAEL On its own, the spider is quite harmless. But the catalyst with which I spiked the staffroom tea makes the venom deadly. I'll take that. [*He seizes the Head's cane.*]

THE HEAD Finish with me, I beg you.   135

MICHAEL Not after the way you dealt with Ophelia. Your agony will be overwhelming. You have just a few minutes, the only part of your body not paralysed is the larynx. Now talk.

Exit MICHAEL *with Ophelia's corpse.*

Scene 6

1964   Speech Day.

THE HEAD unfreezes and addresses the audience.

THE HEAD   Well, the Hutchinson Prize for Expertise in Biology   140
Practical – well done again, Owen – brings us to the end of
the main part of Prize Giving and leaves only our most
coveted award. The Arnold Riley Prize itself, which goes to
Michael Peters of the Upper Sixth Arts. And I hope I shan't
embarrass Michael too much by saying that the committee   145
meeting to decide who should receive this award was one of
the shortest I have ever had the pleasure of chairing. I know
I can rest assured that when, sadly, Michael leaves us at the
end of term, becomes an Old Boy of the school, an Old
Arnold Rileyonian, and goes on to higher things at the   150
University, he will go forth armed with this book as our
ambassador, representing all our hopes and ideals, symbol-
ized completely in the name of Arnold Riley. Come along,
Michael.

*He beckons an imaginary Michael from the audience, then
turns to meet Michael for Scene 7.*

Understanding the text

1 At what point in the scene does the daydream actually start? How is this
reflected in what is actually being said?
2 Pick out three lines which should make the audience laugh because they
are absurd or impossible to believe.
3 There are moments in the scene when the audience are reminded that
this is not a 'real' James Bond scene but just Michael playing with the idea.
Pick out two such moments.
4 What do we learn about the characters of Michael and the Head in
scene 5? Is this changed or developed in any way in Scene 6? If so, how?

Producing the scene

1 What similarities does Mademoiselle have with the standard James Bond heroine? If you were the director of this play, what suggestions could you give to the actress playing the part on how to change from French assistante to Ophelia Plenty. Consider in particular tone of voice, movement and gesture.

2 Why does Michael's daydream start in the first place? Working in groups of three with one person playing Michael, one playing Mademoiselle and one as a director, experiment with ways of showing the change. Compare the effect of making the change suddenly at the point where the stage direction reads *'Fantasy begins'* or working into it gradually from the start of Mademoiselle's speech.

3 How could the actors be positioned in order to achieve a comic effect on the line: 'Careful, James. The skeleton butt of your .25 Beretta is interfering with the mysterious promise of my folded thighs?' (Lines 77-8.) In pairs, imagine you are posing for a publicity photograph designed to show that the play is a comedy.

4 Design or describe a suitable costume for The Head. Would you consider what your own Headmaster wears as a good choice or is your immediate thought to produce something different? Give reasons for your final choice.

5 The stage direction: *'He rips open Michael's shirt, draws blood with cane'* could be achieved in a number of ways. Suggest two possible methods of dealing with this and weigh up the advantages and disadvantages of each.

6 What effect does the stage direction: *'The Head unfreezes and addresses the audience'* have on that audience? What other devices could you use at this point to help the audience understand that we have shifted in time and place?

Further development

1 What other common subjects of daydreams might be suitable for theatrical treatment along these lines? Prepare a short improvisation in which a character drifts off into a daydream with embarrassing or comic results.

2 Find a space in the room on your own and think of a character from any film or TV adventure series. After one minute's thinking time the

teacher or group leader should clap her hands, at which point you must:
- start improvising as that character
- move around the room in search of someone else from the same film or series (it may be another version of your choice)
- when you find her continue improvising together.

3 A number of stories deal with characters who have some trouble separating fact from fiction. You may know books like *Billy Liar* or *The Secret Life of Walter Mitty*. Invent a character who is an incurable liar or daydreamer. In pairs improvise a scene in which the character has been sent to a psychiatrist and is asked to tell how this trait has got her into trouble. The person playing the psychiatrist can help the scene to develop by asking questions which demand detailed answers.

4 In groups of four to six develop some of the ideas generated in Question 3 into 'flashback' scenes.

5 One of the reasons for the success of *The Golden Pathway Annual* is its use of nostalgia. People seem to love wallowing in memories of their youth! As a whole class, imagine yourselves attending a class reunion in 50 years' time. Remember that memories often become more fantastic than the original event. Remind each other, in your improvisation, of some of the amazing characters and incidents of your school days.

6 Following on from Question 5, researching into what your parents or grandparents remember from their youth could provide you with material for a longer piece of work. It would be interesting, for example, to see if their lives fit into the pattern of life described at the start of this chapter. Are they 'baby boomers'? How do they remember the 1960s? Prepare an improvisation which reflects life in the 1980s as you see it.

7 Characters like The Head are often referred to as 'stock characters' or stereotypes. Consider the way comics, cartoons and many popular comedies depict policemen, mothers-in-law and drunkards. What other characters are often stereotyped? Choose a number of stereotypes and invent a scene in which one or several of them confront 'normal', non-stereotyped people in the real world.

THE BODY
by Nick Darke

CAST (in order of appearance)

3 FARMERS
KENNETH
GRACE
ALICE
MAY
GILBERT
RECTOR
ARCHIE GROSS

10 speaking parts. Doubling possible.

Identifying exactly what it is about something that makes us laugh is very difficult. Sometimes we laugh because we feel a kind of sympathy for the characters; if they are in an unfortunate situation we feel a kind of relief that it is them and not us, although we might remember that we have been in similar situations ourselves. Sometimes we laugh because we enjoy seeing someone get her come-uppance; there is a big difference between seeing a stingy millionaire slip on a banana skin and seeing a frail old lady do so.

The Body is, I think, a completely different kind of comedy. For some strange reason we laugh at the inability of human beings to get things right. Perhaps we feel sympathy for ourselves for being members of such a woefully confused species! The play could be described as a 'black comedy' in that underlying the crazy story-line it is making some very bitter comments, and at the end of the play the comedy seems to dissolve altogether, making us wonder what it was that we were laughing about. It is the story of a village in Cornwall which has an American weapons base as a neighbour. The villagers' lives and interests seem trivial, yet they appear, on the whole, content with their lot. The Americans, on the other hand, are crying out for something interesting to happen in order to justify their presence in such a dull place. When one of the American soldiers literally drops dead with boredom it sets off a chain of events which include conscription of one of the locals to fill his place, the arresting of most of the villagers as communist infiltrators, and a major, possibly apocalyptic, international crisis.

The style of the play

The play moves rapidly from one scene to another and was designed for a simple, easily rearranged set. A group of Farmers act as a Chorus throughout the play and, just like the traditional Chorus in a Greek play, they fill in details, comment on the action and speculate on what will happen next. The characterisation of both the locals and Americans is rather unsubtle – they seem to be stereotypes rather than 'real' people, which makes the play both funnier and more pointed in its message.

The extract

This is the opening section of the play. As you will see a number of characters are introduced in quick succession and the action jumps from one place to another. The play launches straight into the action and clearly the audience will have to be alert in order to take it all in.

Prologue

Three FARMERS *of the parish address the audience.*

FARMERS   We, the farmers of this parish,
  Do admit
  The presence of
  American units
  On our airbase.
  We look out across   5
  Our meadows
  And count
  Nuclear weapons
  Amongst our sheep.
  We speak with one voice   10
  And keep our collective

Mouth on the subject shut.
We have no choice,
We know that.
And we gaze with mild disapproval 15
Upon those who seek their removal.

One of our number, Kenneth, sat with his wife one morning,
before breakfast.

> KENNETH *removes himself from the* FARMERS' *group and
> sits with his wife,* GRACE. *She joints a bullock.*

KENNETH   Grace, I fancy mushrooms for breakfast. 20
GRACE   Then pick some.
KENNETH   I think I might. That's what I was thinking.
GRACE   Did you milk the cows?
KENNETH   Yes.
GRACE   Feed the pigs? 25
KENNETH   Yes.
GRACE   Count the sheep?
KENNETH   Yes.
GRACE   Collect the eggs?
KENNETH   Yes. 30
GRACE   Grease the combine?
KENNETH   I can't grease the combine Grace, not before
   breakfast, on an empty stomach.
GRACE   Then don't leave it for me to do at the last minute. I
   can't reach the nipples. There's nipples on that combine was 35
   put in places a cockroach couldn' reach.
KENNETH   My arms is too thick. Yours is thinner.
GRACE   My bosom get in the way.
KENNETH   Then diet.
GRACE   I aren't goin' on a diet so you dun' ave to grease the 40
   combine.
KENNETH   Good a reason as any.
GRACE   And dun't forget the dance tomorrer night.
KENNETH   Tch!
GRACE   Lookin' forward to that. 45
KENNETH   The best field for pickin' mushrooms on my farm
   backs on to the airforce base.

GRACE Be careful.

KENNETH I tell you what I'll do. I'll keep my bedroom slippers
on. It's a light dew and they won't get wet, and the Yanks   50
will take me for what I am. A plain English farmer.

GRACE Don't bank on it.

KENNETH I'll be as long as it takes me to pick a grain pan full
of mushrooms.

> KENNETH *goes.* GRACE *sits. Music plays, then stops.* GRACE
> *looks at her watch.*

GRACE He's late.   55

> *Music plays again.* GRACE *uncrosses her legs and re-crosses
> them the other way. Music stops. She looks at her watch.*

GRACE He's bin gone a day now. Twenty-four hours. I think
I'm gettin' worried. Soon be time to make enquiries. Start
askin' round a bit.

> *She goes. Music intro to* FARMERS' *song.*

Part one

> *The* FARMERS *of the parish, sing a song.*

FARMERS The farmers of this parish
Would dearly love to tell,   60
All about Mother May
A body and a − well,
Mother May went cocklin',
No, we haven't started right,
To get the yarn out viddy   65
We got to start the night
Before,
When Stanly stuck her bloomers
In the roof to stop the leak,
So she could take the bucket out   70
From underneath.
So now she got the *bucket*

To do with what she like,
And with the *bucket* in er 'and
She set sail on her bike.   75
Bike got a puncture
So she ayved'n in the ditch,
Decide to pick some cockles
From beneath the iron bridge.
Now *this* is where the story start,   80
With the cockles, and the *body*,
And Alice, and the iron bridge,
The bucket, and the . . .

> MRS MAY *and* ALICE *walking marchez sur place.* MRS MAY
> *muddy to the knee and carrying a bucket full of cockles.*

ALICE   Mornin' Mrs May.
MAY   Mornin' Alice.   85
ALICE   Hear the larks?
MAY   Lovely.
ALICE   You'm lookin' rosy Mrs May.
MAY   Thank you.
ALICE   Like you bin stridin against the wind.   90
MAY   Bin over the cliff.
ALICE   You'm muddy half way to the knee.
MAY   Ah. Bin in the mud.
ALICE   And you have in your hand a bucket.
MAY   There now.   95
ALICE   Bin cocklin'?
MAY   Observant Alice.
ALICE   Bin under th'iron bridge?
MAY   Iron bridge Alice yes.
ALICE   Iron bridge is it?   100
MAY   And I've found more'n cockles.
ALICE   People often do, under th'iron bridge.
MAY   I was jabbin' about with me toes in the mud, jabbin'
       about for a cockle,
ALICE   Ez . . .   105
MAY   And me foot oozed on summin soft.
ALICE   Flesh.

MAY   I gived it a prod with me stick and it felt like Stanly's belly.

ALICE   Twad'n Stanly . . .   110

MAY   An' I put me 'and down, and twined me finger in a strand of seaweed.

ALICE   Hair . . .

MAY   'Twas a body, what I found beneath th'iron bridge.

ALICE   Dead?   115

MAY   As a doormat.

     ALICE *stops to consider this and* MAY *stops also.*

ALICE   Stil there is 'e?

MAY   I ab'm brung the bugger 'ome in the bucket.

ALICE   Just the one was it?

MAY   How many do 'e want?   120

ALICE   Better inform an authority ad'n'e?

MAY   I will do Alice, after I've 'ad me photograph took with it.

ALICE   'Ere come Archie Gross. Inform 'e.

MAY   I dun't inform Archie Gross a nothin'. Me an' 'e dun't   125
mix.

ALICE   Inform Gilbert. Policeman.

MAY   I will do Alice. But that there body belong to me. So dun't you go yakkin'.

     ARCHIE GROSS *walking marchez sur place. He carries an empty bucket.*

GROSS   Archie Gross, you're a lucky man. The sun's shinin'   130
and the larks are singin'. You've an empty bucket in your 'and, danglin', by thy side, swingin' fore an' back in time with a loose and easy gait, which is step by step drawin' 'e closer to the cockle beds below the iron bridge. And there id'n nothin' like a bucket fulla cockles in the world, bar a   135
good eggy tart like Tysie make. Aw. Cloud loomin' on the horizon, in the bulbous shape a Mrs May. She bring rain to me, she an' me dun't conglomerate. Look like she bin cocklin', so thass summin I d'know 'bout 'er. Less she knaw 'bout me less she can yack around the parish. And there's   140
Alice with 'er, sprig a blossom brought out be the rain.

They converge.

Mornin' Mrs May.
MAY   So they say.
GROSS [*raising his hat*]   Mornin' Alice.
ALICE   Mornin', Mr Gross.   145
GROSS   Hear the larks?
ALICE   Lovely.
GROSS   Bin for a jaunt?
MAY   There and back. Whass that bucket?
GROSS   Ohh, 'tis a bucket.   150
MAY   I noticed, you carry a bucket.
GROSS   I could say the same about you.
MAY   But I'm on me way back. You'm on your way.
GROSS   Ah, I'm er, goin' to milk the cow.
MAY   Out here?   155
GROSS   I have a cow, by name a Buttercup, who wander.
MAY   I hope she yield a good gallon.

   They pass.

FARMERS [*sing*]   So off they went
   To East and West
   With little said   160
   And love lost less
   Mr Gross had told a fib,
   Proper little whopper
   Mrs May and Alice went
   To winkle out a copper.   165

   GILBERT *stands at the station desk. A pile of dollar bills*
   and a box of popcorn sit on the desk-top. GILBERT *eats*
   popcorn. He closes the book and buttons up his jacket.
   MAY *strides in followed by* ALICE.

GILBERT   Mornin' Mrs May.
MAY   Now thun.
GILBERT   Mornin' Alice.
ALICE   Mmmmmmmmmmmmmmmm.
MAY   Gilbert.   170
ALICE   Mmmmmmmmmmmm.

MAY   Gilbert.

GILBERT   Goin' dance tonight?

MAY   Got summin for 'e. Now listen 'ere boy . . .

ALICE   What dance?   175

GILBERT   Parish 'all.

ALICE   Dance tonight, is there?

MAY   Gilbert . . .

GILBERT   Goin'?

MAY   Gilbert . . .   180

ALICE   Mmmmmmm. Who's playin'?

GILBERT   Manny Cockle and the Big Four Combo.

ALICE   Ooh.

MAY   Gilbert.

ALICE   You gonna take me?   185

GILBERT   Mmmmmmmmm.

MAY   Christ!

ALICE   Cus I got to go now . . .

MAY   Alice will you stop yakkin' maid!

GILBERT   Where to?   190

ALICE   Eat me dinner.

MAY   Gilbert you on duty or no?

GILBERT   What 'e got for dinner?

MAY   GILBERT!

ALICE   Eggy tart.   195

     ALICE *goes.*

MAY   *Now* thun!

GILBERT   Eh?

MAY   I found a dead body cocklin'.

GILBERT   Whass a dead body doin' cocklin'.

MAY   *I* was cocklin', the body was dead.   200

GILBERT   Where to?

MAY   Iron bridge.

GILBERT   Under'n?

MAY   Ez you, under'n.

GILBERT   Hell. Whose body is it?   205

MAY   I dunnaw. E'm washed up more like. Up the estuary, out
the sea.

GILBERT Aw.

MAY You comin' or no?

GILBERT I got 'ave me dinner. 210

MAY Gaw damme boy 'twill be washed out again time you've 'ad your dinner!

GILBERT [*not enthusiastic*] Come on thun.

They go.

FARMERS [*sing*] Gilbert was reluctant,
   To say the very least, 215
   To go and dig up bodies
   Where bodies don't exist.
   But before we carry on with them,
   We've raced a bit ahead,
   We must return to Mr Gross, 220
   Who *at* the cockle beds.

> ARCHIE GROSS *cockling. He sits, removes his boots and rolls his trousers up. Checks the independence of his toes, walks a bit and whistles quietly to himself. Suddenly he plunges his foot into the mud, and feels for a cockle. Then he plunges his other foot, and he is cockling. He sings . . .*

GROSS There is nothing like a cockle . . . We are poor black cockles, who have lost our way . . . Old man cockle . . .Cockles in the night . . .Red cockles in the sunset . . . Once, I had a secret cockle . . . 123 o'clock 4 o'clock cockle, 225 567 o'clock 8 o'clock cockle I'm gonna rock, around, the cockle tonight . . .

> *His foot action turns into the twist and he is carried away. Then he stops, his face changes, and he feels very carefully with his toes. He's found the* BODY.

GROSS Hell.

> *He starts to edge his feet horizontally along the* BODY, *stopping at significance places. At last he gets to the head.*

Body.

He feels some more.

Dead. Damme. Now what. Shift'n. Handcart. Take'n 230
church. Inform the rector.

>GROSS *goes off. He leaves the* BODY *lying there. The* BODY
is covered from head to toe with mud.

FARMERS [*sing*] Now this is where our story start
 To gather its momentum,
 Mr Gross and handcart
 Were there and back in no time. 235

>GROSS *comes back with a handcart. He lifts the* BODY *on
and off as they sing.*

The body lifted off the flats
And placed with haste
Upon the trap.
Mrs May, with rumblin' gait,
Arrived with Gilbert, 240
A mite too late.

>MRS MAY *and* GILBERT *arrive on the scene, panting. She
looks around her, conducts the proceedings like a military
exercise.*

MAY Take your boots and stockin's off boy.
GILBERT Eh?

>*She hitches her skirts and plunges her foot in the mud.*

MAY Plunge your foot in.
GILBERT Eh? 245
MAY Got 'ome 'twas rainin'. Said to Stanly, 'Where's me
bloomers?' 'E said, 'Stoppin' up the leak in the roof.' I said,
'Proper job, cockles for tea.' Plunge your foot in boy.

>*She plunges her other foot.*

This is the spot. He'm down 'ere.

>*She feels about. No* BODY.

Damme e'm sunk. 250
GILBERT Eh?
MAY Take your trousers off boy.

GILBERT [*taking off his trousers*] Eh?

MAY 'E've gone deep. 'Ave to probe a bit.

GILBERT Who's the policeman around 'ere.   255

MAY *There* now.

GILBERT What now?

MAY That there body . . .'s vanished.

GILBERT Gyat. Twad'n never there. 'Tis a figment.

MAY Praise the lord! E'm a Lazarus! E've took up his bed an' 260
walked! Advance with me Gilbert! To the rector!

> *And she's gone.* GILBERT *picks up his trousers and follows.*
> ARCHIE GROSS, *pulling his hand cart.*

FARMERS [*sing*] With flying skirt
And rolling lurch
She forged a path
Toward the church   265
With Gilbert, close behind.
Over hill
And down the dip,
Archie Gross
Cracked his whip   270
And galloped with his find.

GROSS Archie Gross, you'm a lucky man. You set out this
mornin' with nothin' more in mind 'n' a handsome bucket
fulla cockles, and here y'are returnin' 'ome with a cartload a
dead body! Hero a the parish! I'll have 'em all yakkin'. An' 275
Mrs May steamin' like a silage pit for lettin' a dead body
through her toes while jabbin' for a cockle beneath the iron
bridge. She think she'm the big I am, but who found the
body!

> *The* BODY *slips off the back of the cart.*

FARMERS [*sing*] No sooner had he said those words,   280
He reached an incline in the road,
Steeper steeper climbed the cart,
And the body slipped off onto the path.

> *The church. The* RECTOR *stands by the lych gate dressed as
> a Chinaman.* ARCHIE *arrives with his empty cart.*

ARCHIE   Rector! I see you're dressed as a Chinaman.
RECTOR   Observant Archie.   285
ARCHIE   And the church seem somewhat altered.
RECTOR   On the outside.
ARCHIE   Now thun.
RECTOR   The nave is exactly as you might remember it.
ARCHIE   Got summin show 'e.   290
RECTOR   You see Archie it started with the fund raisin'.
ARCHIE   Twad'n me who stripped the lead off the steeple.
RECTOR   No 'twas the October gale.
ARCHIE   I lost a dutch barn in that one . . . now look 'ere look,
   in the 'and cart . . .   295
RECTOR   I said to Jack Steeple the steeplejack that steeple,
   Jack, is leakin'. Jack Steeple looked at me and then 'e eyed
   the steeple. Rector, said Jack, the leak in that steeple is
   gonna take some stoppin'. That steeple's bent. I could erect
   a pagoda cheaper. A pagoda said I. Aye said Jack. A   300
   pagoda. I looked at Jack, then I eyed the steeple. All the
   while my 'and clasped the forty seb'm an'sixpence, the
   parish response to my appeal, includin' bingo, and I said to
   meself, so Jack couldn' 'ear, nuts. For all the attention I get
   on a Sunday mornin' I might as well be a Chinaman, so here 305
   I am, pagoda, Chinese cassock wi' dragons on, and pointed
   hat. And do you know Archie? You're the first bugger who's
   noticed.
ARCHIE   Then rector 'tis your lucky day. There's a body in the
   back a that cart!   310
RECTOR   Lead me to it!
ARCHIE   Follow.

> ARCHIE *leads the* RECTOR *round to the back of the cart. The*
> *cart is empty.*

Aw. Aw my gor.
RECTOR   Dearodear.
ARCHIE   I tell 'e Rector 'e was 'ere! Dead as a doormat, lyin' in 315
   the back a the cart!
RECTOR   Come inside the pagoda Archie, an' I'll relieve 'e of a
   sin or two, you'm clearly in need of spiritual aid.
GROSS   'Tis Mrs May. She'm a witch.

RECTOR Mrs May is a stalwart of the parish.   320
GROSS She'll stop a pig bleedin' a mile off, I seed 'er do it!
RECTOR She has a shiny pew, through constant use Archie,
  I'm surprised you found your way here.
GROSS She spirited the bugger off the cart, set the parish
  yakkin!   325

Understanding the text

1 Pick out six examples of where the playwright has tried to capture the accent of the local characters. Give a reason why this might be important in this first scene. What immediate effect does it have on the reader or audience?

2 How would you describe the relationship between Mrs May and Archie Gross as it is outlined in this opening scene? What impression do you get of:
  • their age?
  • their position in the community?
  • their opinion of each other?

3 What sort of character is Gilbert? Is there anything about his appearance on the stage that suggests we shouldn't take him too seriously as a policeman?

4 Explain, in your own words, why the Rector is dressed as a Chinaman? Look at Archie's first comment to him. What does this suggest to you about the characters in this village and Archie in particular?

5 What do you understand by the word 'stereotype'? Make a list of the qualities you would expect to see in:
  • a stereotyped farmer or 'yokel'
  • a stereotyped policeman
  • a stereotyped village gossip.
Find lines in the script, or make up some lines that you think fit such a characterisation well.

Producing the scene

1 Draw a picture of or describe the three farmers in order to show how you would use costume and make-up to create a stereotype. What advice could you give the actors about movement, mannerisms and tone of voice to help bring your drawing to life?

2 Design a costume for the Rector. What problems might you face if you had to actually make such a costume?

3 List at least four properties (props) that you would need to find in order to produce this scene, and design them. Say who they would be used by and whether you think they are the sort of things that could be found or would have to be specially made.

4 List the different places around the village that need to be shown in these opening scenes. How could you suggest each one simply and arrange the stage so that you could move from one piece of action to the next without slowing down the pace of the scene?

5 No lights are specified for this scene, but using lights might help the audience to understand when the action is shifting in terms of time and place. Look at your answer to Question 4 and suggest what sort of lights could be used and where in order to make the scene clearer.

6 Look carefully at the scene where Archie discovers the body. How could you achieve this on stage? (Think particularly about whether the body needs to be concealed and if so, how this could be done.) Act out the scene, experimenting with the timing. How long should Archie do the twist before he finds the body? How quickly should be realise what he has found?

7 Much of the comedy in this scene seems to come from incongruity. the characters often react to things in an unexpected and inappropriate way. Pick out three lines or incidents which you think show this and suggest how the actors on stage could act in order to accentuate the comedy. Try out your suggestions in action to test if they work.

8 What sort of music would you choose for the links in this scene if it wasn't possible to have a live band?

Further development

1 Although it is suggested that the Farmers sing their lines, another technique might be to use choral speech. Pick at least one of their speeches and experiment with ways of producing it as a chorus. Experiment with ways of breaking the speech up so that some lines are spoken by all three Farmers but others are spoken individually. Try exaggerating the accents, rhythm, rhyme and tones of voice to make it funnier.

2 In groups of three or four invent a scene in which the characters are doing something very ordinary, say, fishing, working in a factory or sitting in a launderette. Developing the idea of choral speech, write and present a

commentary on the action. Perhaps, at some point, something extraordinary happens. Rather than being shocked the characters react calmly and comment on it through the use of choral speech.

3 The scene in the police station could be made to be very funny. It works by both Mrs May and Alice trying to talk to Gilbert about two completely different things. Divide into groups of three and improvise a scene in which A is trying to tell B something extremely important. However, B is more interested in carrying on a trivial conversation with C. This could be further developed into a scene in which all three characters are saying something different and not paying attention to whether or not they are being listened to. Devise a way of ending such an improvisation in which the characters realise that what they have said hasn't been heard.

4 *The Body* is a play which tries to make some very serious points through using comedy. Can you think of any television programmes or films which do the same? In groups decide on an issue which you feel strongly about. Devise a scene in which you make serious points about the issue by using comedy.

5 Some of the comedy in the play seems to come purely from the way the characters talk. How aware are you of your own accent? Have you ever heard anyone try to mimic it, if so, what sort of things have they emphasised? Imagine that the BBC have decided to set a series in your area which depicts everyday life in a comic way by over-emphasising the local accent. Either act out the scene as you think they might do it, or improvise a scene in which you are protesting to the director about the way local characters are portrayed. With the help of the class teacher it could be interesting to devise a confrontation between the actors in the series and the locals which illustrates some of the attitudes to regional accents and ways of life.

THE TAMING OF THE SHREW

by William Shakespeare

CAST (in order of appearance)

BIONDELLO
LUCENTIO
BIANCA
GREMIO
PETRUCHIO
KATE
VINCENTIO
* GRUMIO
PEDANT
BAPTISTA
TRANIO
* OFFICER
* ATTENDANTS AND SERVANTS

10 speaking parts. Doubling possible.
* non-speaking parts.

This play remains one of Shakespeare's most popular comedies although it is also one of the most criticised. Its central story concerns how a young man – Petruchio – marries a headstrong young woman – Katherina (Kate) – as a bet. All the men in the town are terrified of Kate, who shows herself to be highly independent in a period when women were expected to be totally subservient. Petruchio, however, is arrogant enough to believe that he can 'tame' her. On their first meeting she tries various tricks to frighten him away, but he treats her insults as tokens of love and insists on an early marriage. Her father, Baptista, is delighted to have her off his hands and the incredulous Kate finds herself taken off by Petruchio to his country house. Her 'taming' is achieved by a series of psychological assaults and tricks. At the end of the play she demonstrates her love for her husband in a speech which appears to suggest that she is now prepared to be an obedient wife. Everyone is amazed.

In recent years *The Taming of the Shrew* has been branded a chauvinistic play, the harsh humour of which reflects an age in which women had less freedom then they do now. But we should not forget that situation comedies today cast women in the stereotyped role of the tyrant (think of all those mother-in-law jokes on TV!). We live, after all, in a society in which wife beating still exists. Was a woman's lot really tougher in Shakespeare's time? Maybe men still like to see themselves as 'taming' women in the way Petruchio does.

Perhaps the most controversial part of the play for a twentieth century audience is Kate's statement of wifely obedience in the final scene of the play, where she seems to be saying that a woman's role in a marriage should be totally subservient. Faced with this, some people prefer to seek an alternative interpretation. They might contrast the superficial romance between Kate's sister (Bianca) and Lucentio, and the true love that develops between Kate and Petruchio. The individual reader or theatre-goer can interpret what Shakespeare wrote however she likes. The headache for the director who decides to put on *The Taming of the Shrew* is how to present the play without offending modern — and in particular female — audiences.

The style of the play

In many ways the strengths of the play lie not so much in the creation of believable characters as in the complex plot which sets up all sorts of traps and situations from which the characters have either to escape themselves or be rescued. In this sense it is a forerunner of farce and the modern 'situation comedy' that can be seen on television almost every night.

The extract

Lucentio is a young man who has gone to Padua to study but has fallen in love with Bianca. In order to woo her he disguises himself as her schoolmaster and calls himself Cambio. He instructs his servant, Tranio, to take his own place in the town. So Cambio is really Lucentio and the person who says he is Lucentio is really his servant, Tranio. Gremio is a rival suitor to Bianca; Biondello is another of Lucentio's servants who has pledged to keep his master's secret. Baptista is Bianca's father, and Grumio is Vincentio's servant. In order to give himself more credibility in the town, Lucentio has persuaded a travelling Pedant to pretend he is his father,

Vincentio. In this scene the real Vincentio arrives in the town to see his son, having met Petruchio and Kate on the road. This is the penultimate scene of the play in which all the various deceptions and disguises are finally exposed.

———————

[ACT V

Scene I *Padua. The street in front of Lucentio's house.*]

> *Enter* BIONDELLO, LUCENTIO [*as* CAMBIO], *and* BIANCA; GREMIO *is out before.*

BIONDELLO Softly and swiftly, sir, for the priest is ready.
LUCENTIO I fly, Biondello. But they may chance to need thee
at home; therefore leave us.

> *Exit* [*with* BIANCA].

BIONDELLO Nay, faith, I'll see the church a your back, and
then come back to my master's as soon as I can. [*Exit.*]   5
GREMIO I marvel Cambio comes not all this while.

> *Enter* PETRUCHIO, KATE, VINCENTIO, [*and*] GRUMIO, *with*
> ATTENDANTS.

PETRUCHIO Sir, here's the door, this is Lucentio's house.
My father's bears more toward the marketplace;
Thither must I, and here I leave you, sir.
VINCENTIO You shall not choose but drink before you go.   10
I think I shall command your welcome here,
And by all likelihood some cheer is toward. [*Knock*].
GREMIO They're busy within. You were best knock louder.

> PEDANT [*as* VINCENTIO] *looks out of the window* [*above*].

PEDANT What's he that knocks as he would beat down the
gate?   15
VINCENTIO Is Signior Lucentio within, sir?
PEDANT He's within, sir, but not to be spoken withal.

line 17 *withal* with

VINCENTIO   What if a man bring him a hundred pound or two,
to make merry withal?

PEDANT   Keep your hundred pounds to yourself; he shall need   20
none so long as I live.

PETRUCHIO   Nay, I told you your son was well beloved in
Padua. Do you hear, sir? To leave frivolous circumstances, I
pray you tell Signior Lucentio that his father is come from
Pisa and is here at the door to speak with him.   25

PEDANT   Thou liest. His father is come from Padua and here
looking out at the window.

VINCENTIO   Art thou his father?

PEDANT   Ay sir, so his mother says, if I may believe her.

PETRUCHIO [To VINCENTIO]   Why how now, gentleman? Why   30
this is flat knavery, to take upon you another man's name.

PEDANT   Lay hands on the villain. I believe 'a means to cozen
somebody in this city under my countenance.

   Enter BIONDELLO.

BIONDELLO   I have seen them in the church together; God send
'em good shipping! But who is here? Mine old master,   35
Vincentio! Now we are undone and brought to nothing.

VINCENTIO   Come hither, crack-hemp.

BIONDELLO   I hope I may choose, sir.

VINCENTIO   Come hither, you rogue. What, have you forgot
me?   40

BIONDELLO   Forgot you? No, sir. I could not forget you, for I
never saw you before in all my life.

VINCENTIO   What, you notorious villain, didst thou never see
thy master's father, Vincentio?

BIONDELLO   What, my old worshipful old master? Yes, marry,   45
sir, see where he looks out of the window.

VINCENTIO   Is't so, indeed? [*He beats* BIONDELLO.]

BIONDELLO   Help, help, help! Here's a madman will murder
me. [*Exit.*]

line 31   *flat*   complete
line 32   *'a*   he
line 32   *cozen*   trick
line 37   *crack-hemp*   villain

PEDANT   Help, son! Help, Signior Baptista! [*Exit from above.*]   50
PETRUCHIO   Prithee, Kate, let's stand aside and see the end of
this controversy. [*They stand aside.*]

> Enter PEDANT [*below*] *with* SERVANTS, BAPTISTA, [*and*]
> TRANIO[*as* LUCENTIO].

TRANIO   Sir, what are you that offer to beat my servant?
VINCENTIO   What am I, sir? Nay, what are you, sir? O
immortal gods! O fine villain! A silken doublet, a velvet   55
horse, a scarlet cloak, and a copatain hat! O, I am undone, I
am undone! While I play the good husband at home, my
son and my servant spend all at the university.
TRANIO   How now, what's the matter?
BAPTISTA   What, is the man lunatic?   60
TRANIO   Sir, you seem a sober ancient gentleman by your
habit, but your words show you a madman. Why sir, what
'cerns it you if I wear pearl and gold? I thank my good
father, I am able to maintain it.
VINCENTIO   Thy father! O villain, he is a sailmaker in   65
Bergamo.
BAPTISTA   You mistake, sir, you mistake, sir. Pray, what do
you think is his name?
VINCENTIO   His name! As if I knew not his name! I have
brought him up ever since he was three years old, and his   70
name is Tranio.
PEDANT   Away, away, mad ass! His name is Lucentio, and he
is mine only son and heir to the lands of me, Signior
Vincentio.
VINCENTIO   Lucentio! O he hath murd'red his master. Lay   75
hold on him, I charge you in the Duke's name. O my son,
my son! Tell me, thou villain, where is my son Lucentio?
TRANIO   Call forth an officer. [*Enter an* OFFICER] Carry this
mad knave to the jail. Father Baptista, I charge you see that
he be forthcoming.   80
VINCENTIO   Carry me to the jail!
GREMIO   Stay, officer. He shall not go to prison.

line 56   *copatain*   tall and conical
line 62   *habit*   manner

BAPTISTA   Talk not, Signior Gremio. I say he shall go to prison.
GREMIO   Take heed, Signior Baptista, lest you be cony-catched
  in this business. I dare swear this is the right Vincentio.   85
PEDANT   Swear, if thou dar'st.
GREMIO   Nay, I dare not swear it.
TRANIO   Then thou wert best say that I am not Lucentio.
GREMIO   Yes, I know thee to be Signior Lucentio.
BAPTISTA   Away with the dotard, to the jail with him!   90
VINCENTIO   Thus strangers may be haled and abused. O
  monstrous villain!

    Enter BIONDELLO, LUCENTIO, *and* BIANCA.

BIONDELLO   Oh we are spoiled – and yonder he is. Deny him,
  forswear him, or else we are all undone.

    Exit BIONDELLO, TRANIO, *and* PEDANT *as fast as may be.*

LUCENTIO   Pardon, sweet father. [*Kneel.*]
VINCENTIO   Lives my sweet son?   95
BIANCA   Pardon, dear father.
BAPTISTA   How has thou offended?
  Where is Lucentio?
LUCENTIO   Here's Lucentio,
  Right son to the right Vincentio,
  That have by marriage made thy daughter mine
  While counterfeit supposes bleared thine eyne.   100
GREMIO   Here's packing, with a witness, to deceive us all!
VINCENTIO   Where is that damned villain Tranio
  That faced and braved me in this matter so?
BAPTISTA   Why, tell me, is not this my Cambio?
BIANCA   Cambio is changed into Lucentio.   105
LUCENTIO   Love wrought these miracles. Bianca's love
  Made me exchange my state with Tranio
  While he did bear my countenance in the town,

line 84 *cony-catched*   tricked
line 90 *dotard*   old fool
line 91 *haled*   pulled about
line 100 *supposes*   pretences
line 100 *eyne*   eyes
line 101 *packing, with a witness*   flagrant deceit

And happily I have arrived at the last
Unto the wished haven of my bliss.   110
What Tranio did, myself enforced him to.
Then pardon him, sweet father, for my sake.

VINCENTIO   I'll slit the villain's nose that would have sent me
to the jail.

BAPTISTA [*To* LUCENTIO] But do you hear, sir? Have you   115
married my daughter without asking my good will?

VINCENTIO   Fear not, Baptista; we will content you, go to. But
I will in, to be revenged for this villainy. [*Exit.*]

BAPTISTA   And I, to sound the depth of this knavery. [*Exit.*]

LUCENTIO   Look not pale, Bianca. Thy father will not frown.   120
[*Exeunt* (LUCENTIO *and* BIANCA).]

GREMIO   My cake is dough, but I'll in among the rest
Out of hope of all but my share of the feast. [*Exit.*]

KATE   Husband, let's follow, to see the end of this ado.

PETRUCHIO   First kiss me, Kate, and we will.   125

KATE   What, in the midst of the street?

PETRUCHIO   What, art thou ashamed of me?

KATE   No sir, God forbid, but ashamed to kiss.

PETRUCHIO   Why, then let's home again. [*To* GRUMIO] Come
sirrah, let's away.   130

KATE   Nay, I will give thee a kiss. Now pray thee, love, stay.

PETRUCHIO   Is not this well? Come, my sweet Kate. Better once
than never, for never too late. [*Exeunt.*]

line 121 *My cake is dough*   my plans have failed

Understanding the text

1 Draw a diagram which shows the names of all the characters in this
scene and how they are connected to each other. This is a bit like drawing
a family tree (only possibly more complicated!).
2 Where are Lucentio and Bianca going at the start of this scene?
3 Pick out the exact moment at which the scene climaxes, that is, the
moment when the problem is at its most acute. How is it resolved in the
script? State, in your own words, what each character intends to do next.

4 Go through the extract and pick out all of the insults which people throw at each other. (Shakespeare had a vast repertoire of imaginative insults which it is well worth researching into.) Do these add comedy or are they spiteful?

5 In what ways do you think this scene is like some situation comedies you know from television?

Producing the scene

1 What requirements should a set design meet for this scene? Read it through again carefully and note the actual structure that needs to be present. Sketch a design which would meet these requirements.

2 Try to work out ways of moving the characters around in this scene. You could do this either by drawing a plan view of the set you sketched in Question 1 and using letters or coloured dots to represent the characters, or, even better, by marking out a space on the floor to represent the set and working out the movements in groups.

3 Where would you place Kate and Petruchio after the stage direction 'They stand aside' in line 52? Although they only play a small part in this scene they are important characters in the play as a whole. What advice would you give them about how to act or react in this scene?

4 A scene such as this in which people are pretending to be someone else can be very confusing for an audience. If you had to direct this scene are there any methods you could use that might help the audience follow it more easily? Characters could use different voices, movements or facial expressions depending on whether they are addressing a character whom they are trying to take in, or the audience (who are aware of the deception that is taking place). Choose a section of no more than 20 lines from the extract (lines 34–52 would be particularly suitable) and make detailed notes as to how you would direct that section.

5 Find out what a 'double take' is. Find a point in the extract where this device could be used to good comic effect.

6 Look carefully at the part Kate and Petruchio play in this scene. What do we learn of their individual characters and their relationship here? Re-read the last ten lines in particular. She calls him 'husband', but do they behave as husband and wife? Either rehearse this short section or discuss how it might be used to show a growing tenderness between the two of them.

Further development

1 Divide into groups of three. A is a lawyer who has been given the job of handing over a large inheritance to a dead millionaire's next-of-kin. B and C turn up both claiming that title. Improvise the scene in the lawyer's office as B and C try to convince A of their claims.

2 Your parents have gone away and left you in charge of the house, trusting you to keep an eye on things. You take this opportunity to have a party (just a little one!) but just as it is in full swing your parents unexpectedly return. Improvise the scene where they appear.

3 Kate and Petruchio have, until this point, had a stormy relationship. Perhaps it is in this scene that they discover, by watching the confused events taking place, that they have the same sense of humour and this leads them to develop more affection for each other. In pairs, improvise an argument between two people who have been forced by circumstances to live with each other. At some point a third person enters and does something that changes the atmosphere from tension to relief. Try to launch into this without planning but rely on your powers of invention to provide an idea on the spur of the moment.

4 With the help of your teacher, play a variation of the game 'Keeper of the Gate' to generate ideas on secrets. This might work as follows. The whole group sits in a semi-circle and one volunteer takes up position in the middle. It is her job to guard an imaginary door. Only she knows what is behind the door and she is anxious that no one else should find out. Students sitting in the semi-circle take it in turns to approach the doorkeeper and try to present a convincing argument as to why they should be let through and discuss what's inside. The doorkeeper must try to give logical and believable reasons not to allow them in. Whoever runs out of logical, reasonable arguments first is the loser.

5 Some of the ideas generated in Question 4 could help you to develop a scene in which each character has a secret which she is desperately trying to keep, although the situation is making it increasingly difficult for her to do so.

6 At the end of the play Kate amazes all who knew her before she married Petruchio by seeming so different. Write or improvise a story in which a notorious character in your class seems to undergo an astonishing change. Has it really happened or are they leading you on?

CANDLEFORD

by Keith Dewhurst

CAST (in order of appearance)

BEN
TOM
LAURA
MRS GUBBINS
BILL
SOLOMON
BAVOUR
BROWN

8 speaking parts. No doubling.

Candleford was first presented at The National Theatre in 1979 as the second half of a rather unusual project. The first half of the project had been presented a year earlier. Two plays were adapted from a trilogy of novels by Flora Thompson called *Lark Rise to Candleford*. The first play, simply called *Lark Rise*, takes place on the first day of the harvest. All the action takes place in the one day. Flora Thompson herself appears in the play as a little girl called Laura. In the second play, *Candleford*, Laura has grown old enough to go away to work in the post office and smithy of a neighbouring village. As *Lark Rise* is set on a hot summer's day, so *Candleford* is set on a cold winter's one. Both plays use folk songs to add to the atmosphere and make them more entertaining.

Making plays from novels isn't a particularly new idea. As you will probably know, many films are also made from original novels. *Lark Rise to Candleford* posed a tricky problem, though, in that there isn't really any story to it. The book is about different aspects of life in a small group of villages in Oxfordshire at the end of the last century, and the reader's attention is kept not by the unfolding of a plot but by the colourful descriptions of the characters and their lives. The problem with dramatising such a book is that most pieces of theatre rely on 'dramatic tension' – the audience watches and listens because it wants to know what will happen next. With *Lark Rise to Candleford* a way had to be found of giving life to Flora Thompson's descriptions and recreating the atmosphere of village life. Most important the audience would have to be made to feel a part of the village.

The style of the play

Keith Dewhurst's answer to the problem was to write the plays so that they could be performed as 'promenade productions' – that is to say that rather than having the audience seated looking forward onto a stage, or even having the action going on in the middle of the audience (theatre in the round) the audience are left to wander around with the action happening amongst them. Such a technique aimed to create an impression of life going on in the village just as Flora Thompson had described it, with the audience watching like invisible ghosts. Acting in a play like this requires enormous concentration on the part of the actors who have to make space for themselves and catch the audience's attention whilst trying to capture a sense of authenticity in the portrayal of their characters. Of course, from an audience's point of view, also, the experience is quite demanding as you have to keep moving around. Keith Dewhurst sums up the experience like this: 'No one sees all the play, although if it can be heard it can be followed, and some emotions must be read off the faces of other spectators. In a way each person is his or her own television camera, and at the same time part of the show.'

The extract

One of the post women, Mrs Macey, has been called away to attend to her sick husband. This gives the locals something to gossip about, as does the fact that today is the day of the hunt. The action takes place in and around the village post office and whilst not very much actually happens the succession of local characters provides plenty of interest.

[BEN TROLLOPE *and* TOM ASHLEY *cross the green. They are old army pensioners.* BEN *is a tall, upright old fellow with a neat, well-brushed appearance and clear straight gaze.* TOM *is more retiring, a little shrunken, bent and wizened*]

BEN   Pick your feet up, soldier. Pick 'em up.

TOM   I'm freezin' cold.

BEN   I know you're a-freezing, Tom. I know it. [*They enter the post office*]

BEN   Afternoon, missy.   5

LAURA   Afternoon, Mr Trollope. Didn't expect to see you in this snow, Mr Ashley.

TOM   Didn't expect to see myself.

LAURA   When were you here last?

TOM   Three month ago.   10

BEN   Last time us pensions were due. [*They present their books.* LAURA *checks them. There is money in the counter drawer*] Them's due again today and I said today's the day we should collect 'em!

TOM   I said, 'Look here, I've got my mending and cooking to   15
do', but being the Sergeant he says, 'Quick march'.

LAURA   How's your garden in all this?

BEN   Geraniums and fuschias is indoors; t'others takes their chance. Interested in flowers, aren't you, missy?

LAURA   Oh, yes.   20

BEN   Aye.

LAURA   I like the way you line yours up, like soldiers.

TOM   That's what we was, missy!

BEN   Seeing as you like flowers you'd be head over heels with India, wouldn't she, Tom, especially the Himalayas.   25

LAURA   Oh, but I know! Northward of the great plains of India, and along the whole extent, towers the sublime mountain region of the Himalayas, ascending gradually until it terminates in a long range of summits wrapped in perpetual snow. . . .   30

BEN   Have you learned that by heart?

LAURA   From a book at school.

BEN   Well, then, you deserve to go there yourself, for I never saw anything like it, never in my life! Great sheets of scarlet as close-packed as they grasses on the Green, and primulas   35
and lilies and things such as you only see here in a hothouse, and rising right out of 'em, great mountains all covered with snow. Ah! 'Twas a sight – a sight! And what scents, eh?

What scents and smells! That's why we rented our cottage – 'cause it had jessamine over the door.   40

TOM   Aye. The scent of jessamine.

BEN   India, missy, India. I wake up sometimes and think I've heard the bugle. I think I'll smell all the smells and blink my eyes in the glare and see the mutineers come at us. Horsemen in the dust.   45

TOM   Sergeant. I want my mother, Sergeant.

BEN   Too late, son. Face your front and fire on the young gentleman's command. [*Silence.* LAURA *watches them*] Aye. Aye. It seems to get hold of you, like, somehow. [LAURA *gives them their pension money*] Thank you, missy. Good day.   50
[*Music starts, very quietly, as they go. Outside they check*]

TOM   Imagine it; forty year ago a wench jilted me so I took the Queen's shilling. I'd not be that downcast now.

BEN   Haven't you left that curry on the hob?

TOM   Aye; and I wish we were back in India, with a bit of hot   55
sun.

BEN   T'ain't no good wishing, Tom. We've had our day and that day's over. We shan't see India no more.

[BEN *and* TOM *sing their 'Old Soldier's Song'*. BEN *the first verse,* TOM *the second, both the chorus*]

SONG   I left my native country
   I left my native home   60
   To wear a soldier's tunic
   And preserve the good Queen's throne.
   I travelled out to India, the mutiny to quell.
   I have visited sweet paradise, and seen the gates of hell.

CHORUS   When we wore the scarlet and the blue,   65
   We took the old Queen's shilling
   When the Empire days were new.
   Forward into battle, don't you hear the bugle call.
   Raise the tattered standard and let me like a soldier fall.

   I've seen the Himalayas and I've been to Katmandu,   70
   Seen sights to dazzle Solomon,
   The tales I could tell you.

From Banbury to Bombay,
All the good times have gone by,
Now don't believe the man who says, 'old soldiers never   75
  die'.

Chorus

> [*They march off, as smartly as they can manage.*
> MRS GUBBINS *crosses the Green.*
> BILL, SOLOMON *and* BAVOUR *are passing in and out of the*
> *forge*]

BILL   Whoa-up, lads!
BAVOUR   Afternoon, Mrs Gubbins.
MRS GUBBINS   Huh!
SOLOMON [*Singing*]   And huh say all of us!   80
  For she's a grumpy old sow like
  For she's a grumpy old sow like.
MRS GUBBINS [*Arriving at the post office*]   No sign of the post
  yet?
LAURA   No.   85
MRS GUBBINS   Huh!
MRS GUBBINS   Any news?
LAURA   News?
MRS GUBBINS   You know.
LAURA   I don't.   90
MRS GUBBINS   Mrs Macey.
LAURA   Oh. . . .!
MRS GUBBINS   If there is, tell us now afore he comes.
LAURA   No. I mean there isn't. I mean, so far as I know there's
  been no word. Wait a minute – here he is now.   95

> [POSTMAN BROWN *crosses the Green*]

BROWN   'Deep and wide. . . .'
SMITHS   Praise the Lord. Jesus saves. Hallelujah.

> [BROWN *waves cheerily to the smiths and enters the post*
> *office*]

BROWN   Afternoon, young Laura.

LAURA Afternoon, Mr Brown.

BROWN Mrs Gubbins.   100

MRS GUBBINS Huh!

BROWN How was your delivery?

LAURA Fine.

BROWN I knew you'd not flinch. [BROWN *empties the postbag and they set to work*] Tell you what.   105

LAURA What?

BROWN As I was a-comin' up the Fordlow Lane, I see'd that there's them old gippos again.

MRS GUBBINS Gippos?

BROWN Aye. Caravans and all!   110

MRS GUBBINS Time they was routed out o'them places, the 'ole stinkin' lot of 'em. If a poor man so much as looks at a rabbit he soon finds hisself in quod but their pot's never empty.

BROWN There's a lot of people says they eats hedgehogs! 115 Hedgehogs! He! He!

MRS GUBBINS Hedgehogs! Ha! ha! ha!

BROWN Hedgehogs wi' soft prickles!

MRS GUBBINS [*Abruptly stops laughing*] I seed that Mary Merton on the Green.   120

BROWN Eh?

MRS GUBBINS There's summat there as is not as it should be.

BROWN Wind's changed an' all. Come round to the West. I could smell old Jolliffe's muckhill. [*They work.* BROWN *tries to keep his next remark sotto voce to* LAURA] Any – er – any 125 word from Mrs Macey?

MRS GUBBINS What? What's that 'un said?

BROWN Nothing.

MRS GUBBINS Nothing?

BROWN No.   130

MRS GUBBINS Huh!

[*They work*]

MRS GUBBINS [*She holds up a letter*] Ha!

BROWN Eh?

MRS GUBBINS Look us here, now! Miss Mary Merton. To be called for at the post office. Whose handwriting be that? 135

LAURA I don't know.

MRS GUBBINS Certain are you?

LAURA Yes.

MRS GUBBINS Huh!

[*They work*]

BROWN Mrs Gubbins.   140

MRS GUBBINS Uh?

BROWN How long have us knowed each other?

MRS GUBBINS Twenty-five year.

BROWN Thirty.

MRS GUBBINS 'Appen thirty.   145

BROWN Aye, and I'll be jiggered if you've ever spoke very much, except about other folk's business.

MRS GUBBINS You can tell that to Jesus.

BROWN I have found Jesus, Mrs Gubbins, [*Huge pause*] and if I mention you at all, I shall ask Him to help you, not tell 150 tales about you.

MRS GUBBINS Did you or did you not ask young Laura if 'un had heard any word from Mrs Macey?

[BROWN *opens his mouth to deny the charge and then realizes that he cannot.* MRS GUBBINS *chuckles*]

BROWN I can't think what there is for you to laugh at.

MRS GUBBINS You. Rain, hail, sunshine or snow, you're the 155 biggest ole gossip I've ever seed.

BROWN I'm the – No, no! Not so. What it be is, that all sorts o'folk confides in me.

MRS GUBBINS Huh!

BROWN Huh? Look 'ee 'ere. This very morning that 160 Mrs Wardup what lives at the hungry end of the Green taps on her window when she sees me, and my word, but haven't she got worries what with her sister's son not able to stop himself bed-wetting.

MRS GUBBINS Bed-wetting?   165

BROWN Aye.

MRS GUBBINS Fried mice.

BROWN Fried mice?

MRS GUBBINS Fried mice for the supper stops a growed man a-wetting his bed, never mind a nipper.   170

BROWN   Fried mice. Well. I've never heard that one afore, have you, young Laura?

MRS GUBBINS   Huh. [*She sighs and shakes her head at them. She's not surprised. They work.* MRS GUBBINS *finds another interesting letter*]   175

MRS GUBBINS   Hello. Here's one for that Co-lo-nel.

LAURA   Yes. Colonel Scott.

MRS GUBBINS   Co-lo-nel.

LAURA   Colonel.

MRS GUBBINS   Co-lo-nel.   180

LAURA   Colonel.

MRS GUBBINS   Co-lo-nel as plain as the nose on your face. I don't know what they teach 'em at school these days.

[*They work*]

BROWN   Mind you. I have heard of black slugs for warts.

MRS GUBBINS   Slugs?   185

BROWN   Slugs. For warts. You bind 'em on for a day and a night.

MRS GUBBINS   Dead or alive?

BROWN   The slugs? Alive. I saw it done once, twenty odd year ago, by a young chap as sorted parcels at Candleford. [*They*   190 *work*] Mind you; when he took the slug off it were dead.

MRS GUBBINS   What about the wart?

BROWN   Well, no more'n a week after, the young chap's transfer came through. General Post Office, Oxford. I never seed him again.   195

MRS GUBBINS   But did 'un, or did 'un not, charm the wart?

BROWN   Dunno, do I? He still had 'un when he left Candleford.

[MRS GUBBINS *sighs*]

BROWN   Is this 'ere, all the village delivery?

MRS GUBBINS   Aye.   200

LAURA   Yes.

BROWN   I'll be off with 'un then – and come back with the letter-box post. [*On his way out* BROWN *checks*] You'll notice it's a-thawed a bit.

MRS GUBBINS   Eh?   205

BROWN   I said you'll notice it's thawed a bit. Allus the same. I'm jiggered if it's not. Thaws, and just starts to freeze again afore the afternoon delivery. [*Sings*] 'Yes, Jesus loves me. . . .'

[As BROWN *passes the forge the men are finishing their work. They sing as they go into the living room for their tea. It is almost dark again. Lamps are lit. . .*]

Understanding the text

1 List five things that you find out about Ben and Tom through what they say in this scene. For example, we know they are pensioners because they have come to collect their pensions.

2 Part of the playwright's art is to be able to tell an audience not only about the characters in the way you discovered in Question 1, but something about the time and place in which they exist. Pick out three things which are said which show that:
  • the play is set in the country
  • it is not in the present day.
What other bits of information are included in the dialogue here which you think are important for the audience's understanding?

3 There are a number of touches of gentle humour in the scene which give the characters a warmth and make them believable. Pick out any lines that you feel achieve this particularly well. It might be interesting for you to compare the characterisation of rural folk here to that in *The Body*.

4 Look at the discussion between Laura and Mrs Gubbins about how to pronounce the word Colonel. What does this tell us about Laura?

Producing the scene

1 List the different locations mentioned in the scene. Imagine you are producing this play in your school hall. Draw a sketch or diagram showing how you could use its full space to recreate the village and suggest both the inside and outside of the post office and smithy. Bear in mind that the audience, in a promenade performance, can move around but as many as possible should be able to watch each different scene.

2 Suggest as many ways as you can of creating the atmosphere of a really cold day. What techniques could the actors use to help the audience also

feel a part of this cold day? With the help of your teacher divide the class into two groups. Group A should imagine that they have come to watch this play. Group B, as the actors, enter and improvise with Group A to establish the location and the idea of a cold day. What can you say and do to create the scene within a short space of time?

3 Design a costume for either Tom, Ben or Laura and give reasons for your choice of clothes.

4 Imagine you are playing either Brown or Mrs Gubbins. Describe what sort of person you think he/she is and explain how you could use your voice and body to recreate them.

5 Why do you think Tom suddenly says, 'Sergeant, I want my mother, Sergeant,' to which Ben replies, 'Too late, son. Face front and fire on the young gentleman's command.'? What suggestions would you give the actors about how to deliver these lines? Act out this short extract and try to change the atmosphere from that of the post office to that of the front line by changing tone of voice and position.

6 What reasons can you give for the inclusion of 'The Old Soldier's Song'? Given that in a promenade performance the actors are working in amongst the audience consider:

- what problems this might pose for the actors playing Tom and Ben
- how they could stage the song so as actively to help the audience feel the atmosphere of the song's lyrics.

Further development

1 Laura's family live in a neighbouring village. In pairs or small groups, act out a scene in which she goes to visit them. What news would she take from Candleford?

2 As well as being gossips, Brown and Mrs Gubbins have some interesting ideas about medicine. Set up a scene in a hospital which specialises in using 'traditional' cures for ailments. Be as bizarre and imaginative as you like.

3 Bill, Solomon and Bavour are apprentice smiths in the village. Most of their work on this day has come from the local gentry who are off hunting. Write or improvise a scene which shows how the smiths would talk and behave to the hunters.

4 The post office seems to be a good place to catch up on local gossip and meet a cross-section of the local people. Can you suggest any other places in the village which might also be good for 'studying' the locals? Set up an improvisation in such a place and see if, bit by bit, you can invent your own colourful local personalities.

5 Imagine that, at some point, Laura and the others in this scene have their photograph taken. In groups position yourselves to show the relationship between the characters and, as far as possible, their characters and attitudes. Extend the photograph to incude other villagers either mentioned in the play or of your own invention. If each character were allowed to say one line about their life in Candleford, what would it be?

6 The play has a strong air of nostalgia about it. Ben and Tom talk about their former lives in India and life in the village is depicted as being straightforward and enjoyable. Have you ever heard older people going on about 'the good old days'? What sort of things do they say? Think about your own area, town or village and in small groups act out a scene in which a number of old people are reminiscing about days gone by.

7 Following on from Question 6, look carefully at the extract and see if you can find anything that suggests that life in a village 100 years ago may have actually been quite hard. You could do some research of your own into what life was like in your home town in, say, your grandparents' time. See if you can make a piece of theatre that shows that people sometimes think 'the good old days' were better than they actually were. Perhaps your scene could aim to remind them of the real hardships faced.

GREGORY'S GIRL

by Bill Forsyth

CAST (in order of appearance)

CAROL
LIZ
SUSAN
ANN
STEVE
GREGORY

6 speaking parts. Doubling possible.

Gregory's Girl started life as a film but has since been performed in many schools and youth theatres. When the film was first released it quickly achieved enormous success and seemed to represent something new and refreshing in that it wasn't like other teenage love stories. The characters generally seem fallible and therefore much more believable than the idealised youths of American movies. Gregory, for example, makes a very unlikely hero with his gangling walk and inability to do anything well.

The story tells of how the school PE master tries to improve the quality of his desperately bad football team by holding a trial for new players. The only person to reveal any talent, however, is a girl called Dorothy. Neither the players nor the PE teacher like the idea of having a girl in the team, but she is clearly their only hope. The only one who thinks her inclusion in the side is a good idea is Gregory, and it is he, ironically, who loses his place to her. However, Gregory has fallen in love with Dorothy and so doesn't mind. Eventually he manages to summon up enough courage to ask her out. She accepts, but doesn't show up at the appointed time, passing Gregory on, instead, to a friend who fancies him.

The sharpness of the girls in the play as opposed to the slowness and innocence of the boys also makes a refreshing change from stereotypes, though some might argue that girls are dealt with rather thinly in the story. Bill Forsyth says, 'it began to dawn on me that as a "mature person" I was still going through the heartaches and doubts of Gregory twelve years later!' A wonderful thing about theatre and film is that you can watch someone very much like yourself going through awkward or painful experiences that you yourself have been through in real life, but instead of you being hurt or embarrassed by them, the character in the film is. What is painful at first hand can be funny when you are the observer. I call this type of comedy 'the banana skin syndrome'. But far from laughing at Gregory in a cruel way, I think we laugh because we sympathise with him.

The style of the play

When Bill Forsyth originally worked out the story, much of it developed through improvisation. The script has kept an 'improvised' feel to it which in places makes some of the jokes fall a bit flat and seem out of place. On the other hand the short scenes and uncomplicated characters make it easy to add to and alter for one's own purposes. Being originally written for film, the action tends to jump about a lot, and for the theatre it is necessary to combine a number of the scenes. Putting a football match onto a stage is rather more difficult than filming it, of course, and so there are some interesting technical challenges to be met.

The extract

In this extract Gregory tells his best friend about his love for Dorothy. His friend, Steve, however, is much more interested in cooking than in girls, and in a reversal of stereotyped sex roles it is the girls in the class who come to him for advice about their projects.

Scene 6   The cookery class

[CAROL, LIZ, SUSAN, ANN *and others set up the Home Economics room. They are making pastry.*]

CAROL   Did you hear about the trial?
LIZ   Trial?
CAROL   Football trial. Dorothy joined it.
LIZ   And about time too.
SUSAN   Why is it boys are such a physical disaster?   5
CAROL   Apparently Phil wouldn't let her play.

SUSAN Too much to lose I expect.
CAROL Well, she stuck it out and showed him up something
  rotten.
ANN Oh God, not pastry. I hate pastry and it hates me. Give   10
  me a goulash anyday. It doesn't fight back.
CAROL She scored three times with him in goal.
SUSAN Poor Phil.
LIZ Have you seen his moustache?
CAROL Anyway he's got to pick her now.   15
LIZ Men's hair fascinates me. It's so temporary.
ANN Equal parts of Trex and lard. Isn't that it?

  [*The boys are coming in for the lesson. It is a mixed
  lesson.* STEVE *is in first. He is a professional. Already he
  has his bench organised.*]

STEVE Anyone seen Gregory? He's meant to be working with
  me . . . oh dear Lizzie, not the hands. Lay off the hands till
  the last possible minute.   20

  [GREGORY *is late and makes his way through the girls. He
  is trying to be both charming and surreptitious.*]

GREGORY Sorry I'm late.
STEVE Where've you been?
GREGORY Football.
STEVE Playing?
GREGORY No . . . watching. From afar.   25
STEVE Hands!

  [GREGORY *shows him his hands. It is a routine inspection.*]

GREGORY That's just paint there.
STEVE I've got the biscuit mix started, you get on with the
  sponge and put the oven on, four hundred and fifty degrees.
GREGORY Yes, boss.   30

  [SUSAN *approaches* STEVE. *She is wearing a worried look
  and a grotty apron.*]

SUSAN Steve, can you help me out with the pastry mix thing?
GREGORY Hello, Susan.

[GREGORY *is ignored.*]

STEVE   Pastry? What pastry? There's more than one kind you know. Is it rough puff, short crust . . . flaky . . . suet. . . ?

[SUSAN's *face is a blank.*]

Just tell me, what are you making?   35

SUSAN   A meat pie. Margaret's doing the Strudel Soup, and I'm doing the pie. It's the eggs for the pastry that I'm not sure of. . .

STEVE   Strudel Soup, eh? I'd like to try some of that. It's NOODLE soup, and what eggs? You don't put eggs in a   40 pastry. It's 8 ounces flour, 4 ounces margarine. . .

GREGORY   . . . a pinch of salt. . .

STEVE   . . . some salt, mix it up, into the oven, fifteen minutes . . . and that's it, okay? No eggs, no strudels, nothing.

SUSAN   Is that all? That's *simple*, really easy. [*She wanders*   45 *off.*]

STEVE   To think there are five guys in fifth year crying themselves to sleep over that.

GREGORY   Six, if you count the music teacher.

STEVE   Watch your mixing, it goes stiff if you overdo it, thirty seconds is enough. Give me the sugar.   50

GREGORY   It's time *you* were in love. Take your mind off all this for a while. . .

STEVE   Plenty of time for love. I'm going to be a sex maniac first. Start this summer. Get rid of my apron and let my hair down, put love potions in my biscuits. Anyway I want to be   55 rich first, so that I can love something really . . . expensive.

GREGORY   You're daft. You should try it. Love's great.

STEVE   Who told you?

GREGORY   I'm in love. [*He means it. He is abstractedly stirring the sponge mix with his finger.*] I can't eat, I'm awake half   60 the night, when I think about it I feel dizzy. I'm restless . . . it's wonderful.

STEVE   That sounds more like indigestion.

GREGORY   I'm serious.

STEVE   Or maybe you're pregnant, science is making such   65 progress. . . [STEVE *extracts* GREGORY's *finger from the mixing bowl and starts to wipe it clean.*] Come on, who is it? Is it a mature woman? Did you do anything dirty? Did you wash your hands? 70

GREGORY Don't be crude.

STEVE Come on! Who is it?

GREGORY You'll just laugh, and tell people.

STEVE Give us a clue.

GREGORY [*Reluctantly*] It's somebody in the football team. 75

STEVE [*Silent for a moment*] Hey, that's really something. Have you mentioned this to anyone else? Listen, it's probably just a phase . . . is it Andy, no, no . . . is it Pete?

GREGORY Come on! I mean Dorothy, she came into the team last week. She's in 4A . . . she's a wonderful player, she's a 80 *girl*. She goes around with Carol and Susan, she's got long lovely hair, she always looks really clean and fresh, and she smells mmm . . . lovely. Even if you just pass her in the corridor she smells, mmm, gorgeous. . . She's got teeth, lovely teeth, lovely white, white teeth. . . 85

STEVE Oh, *that* Dorothy, the hair . . . the smell . . . the teeth . . . *that* Dorothy.

GREGORY That's her, that's Dorothy.

STEVE The one that took your place in the team.

GREGORY So what. She's a good footballer. She might be a bit 90 light but she's got skill, she's some girl. . .

STEVE Can she cook? Can she do this?

[STEVE *throws the rolled out pastry into the air and juggles with a pizza-maker's flourish.*]

GREGORY [*Being very serious*] When you're in love, things like that don't matter.

STEVE Gimme the margarine. 95

GREGORY Do you think she'll love me back?

STEVE No chance . . . watch that mix! I told you, nice and slowly . . . take it easy. . . [STEVE *takes* GREGORY's *hands in his and guides him through the movements of a nice and easy stir.*] 100

GREGORY What d'you mean no chance?

STEVE No chance.

Understanding the text

1 The dialogue in this scene is very 'naturalistic'. That is, it attempts to capture the way people actually speak rather than being written in a poetic or 'stagy' way. Pick out four lines that you think demonstrate this.
2 What do you learn about Steve in this scene? Consider his talent for cooking and compare it with how the girls appear to be getting on. What point do you think the author is trying to make here?
3 Look closely at the lines written for the girls in this scene. Note down:
- what you learn about them as characters
- what other functions they fulfil in terms of telling the story.

4 Steve suggests that there is 'No chance' of Dorothy loving Gregory. What do we learn about Gregory in this scene that suggests he may be right?

Producing the scene

1 Setting up the cookery class on stage for such a short scene could prove a nuisance. List the minimum number of characters necessary in the scene and draw a plan view of a possible set and the actors' positions on it which could suggest a larger class in action.
2 List as many props as you think necessary to 'set the scene' here, remembering that it will be necessary to move them on and off quickly.
3 In small groups, improvise a number of things that the girls could be doing in the background while Steve and Gregory are talking. What sort of things could be amusing and add to the scene without being too much of a distraction from the main action? Try to take account of their characters as far as you can understand them from the actual script.
4 What do you think the biggest problem might be for the actor playing Steve? Suggest and possibly try out ways of overcoming this.
5 Discuss what you think is meant by the stage direction which describes Gregory's entrance: '*He is trying to be both charming and surreptitious*'. In small groups, use the knowledge you have of Gregory from the introductory notes and this scene itself to experiment with ways of having him enter. Try at least four different types of entrance and then choose the one you feel is most appropriate.
6 Gregory's line 'It's somebody in the football team' (line 75) should be very funny on stage. How could the other actors on stage help make it so?

Further development

1 A famous director once stated that there was no such thing as a small part – only small actors! I think he meant that even though a character may only have a few lines, she is still an integral part of the scene and must be believable. Look carefully at the attitudes of the girls in this scene and invent another scene which tells us more about their characters.

2 Get into pairs and sit back to back. Improvise a telephone call in which one person is desperate to ask the other out but just can't summon up the courage to do so.

3 In different pairs from Question 2 label yourselves A and B. A is rather like the girls in the extract – not particularly shy and not the stereotyped sweet schoolgirl. B is a character more like Gregory – innocent and unsure. Improvise a scene in which B is sitting on a bench. A enters and starts chatting him up.

4 *Gregory's Girl* tries in a number of instances to surprise the audience by presenting characters as being the opposite of or at least different to, their sex stereotype. Make a list of any professions which you would normally associate with one sex or another. Prepare an improvisation in which someone who has set ideas about what sex a particular type of person is going to be is surprised when they encounter someone who is not of the sex they were expecting.

5 In groups write down, as quickly as possible, all the ideas that come into your head in response to the idea of 'first love'. When you have really run out of ideas, look at your list and use it as a resource from which to make a collection of short lines and appropriate visual images which capture the essence of 'first love'. One technique might be to depict (make a tableau of) a number of photographs with a spoken caption for each one. This could be developed into a piece of movement or mime.

6 Steve's line, 'there are five guys in the fifth year crying themselves to sleep over that' (lines 47-8) tells us quite a lot about Susan to whom he is referring at the time. In pairs invent a character and write four essential and interesting pieces of information about her on a slip of paper. The slips are collected in and redistributed around the group. Each pair must now write or improvise a conversation which contains the four pieces of information but sounds as natural as possible.

Activity Chart

The chart on pages 164 and 165 shows the skills developed in the Activities section of each extract.

Across the top of the chart are the extract titles, in order. Down the side are fifteen of the main assessment criteria for drama at first examinations.

You can use the chart as a quick reference aid. With it you can:

- find a particular activity.
- plan longer coursework or project investigations based on particular areas of your syllabus.
- identify the types of activities developed with particular extracts.

The chart is specially helpful if you want to pursue a particular line of investigation, for example costume design. Read across the 'Costume Design' line and you will find all the extracts with activities to help you in your investigation.

The chart is also helpful if you are stuck on a particular activity. It enables you to find similar activities which will help clarify or develop your work.

Finally the chart is helpful if you want to know which extracts to select for particular areas of work in drama.

In the chart the following abbreviations are used:

UT ....Understanding the text
PS ....Producing the scene
FD ....Further development

So, UT 1/2/3 in the square for Characterization under *The Wild Duck* shows that Activities 1, 2 and 3 in the 'Understanding the text' section of *The Wild Duck* all involve work on characterization.

	The Wild Duck	Example	Indians	A Dream Play	She's Dead	Johnson over Jordan	The Spanish Tragedy	The Lucky Ones
Characterization	UT 1/2/3	UT 2	UT 3 PS 6	UT 3	PS 6 FD 6	UT 2/3 PS 4 FD 2	UT 2 FD 6	UT 1/3
Use of Language	UT 4/5/6	UT 1	UT 1/2/4	UT 1/2	UT 2/3/4 FD 5/6		UT 1 PS 6	UT 2
Theatrical Style		UT 3/4	UT 5	UT 4	UT 1	UT 1/4	UT 3/4	UT 4
Set/Props design	PS 1	PS 1/2	PS 1/3		PS 1/2		PS 3/4	PS 1
Lighting and Sound	PS 1	PS 3	PS 4	PS 2/3		PS 4 1/2/3 FD 7	PS 1 FD 4	
Costume Design	PS 2		PS 2	PS 1		PS 4	PS 2	
Movement Work	FD 8	FD 4	PS 6	PS 4/5 FD 6		PS 5	FD 4	PS 5 FD 7
Vocal Work				FD 5	PS 7 5/8	FD 5	FD 4	PS 2
Directing Acting	PS 4/5	PS 4	PS 5		PS 4/5	PS 6/7	PS 5	PS 4
Stage Direction	PS 3/6		PS 6/7	PS 4	PS 3/7/8	PS 7	PS 4	PS 3
Spontaneous Improvisation	FD 1/2	FD 1	FD 2/3	FD 1/2/3	FD 1/2/3	FD 1/2 3/4	FD 1	FD 1/2/3
Prepared Improvisation	FD 3/4/5 6/7	FD 2/3	FD 4/5/6	FD 4/5	FD 4/7	FD 6	FD 2/3/4 5	FD 4/5/6
Script/Creative Writing	FD 4	PS 6 FD 3	FD 4/5/6	FD 4	FD 6	FD 3/6	FD 3/6	FD 5/6
Discussion		FD 4	FD 1	UT 5 PS 6	UT 5 FD 4			PS 6 FD 6/7
Research		FD 2/4	FD 6					

Vinegar Tom	The Country Wife	The Golden Pathway Annual	The Body	The Taming of the Shrew	Candleford	Gregory's Girl
UT 3/4	UT 2/3 FD 1	UT 4 PS 4 FD 3	UT 2/3/4	UT 1/3	UT 1/4 PS 4 FD 4/5	UT 2/3/4 FD 1
UT 1	UT 4	UT 1	UT 1/4	UT 2/4		UT 1
UT 3/5 PS 3	UT 1	UT FD 7	UT 5	UT 5	UT 2/3	
PS 1/2	PS 1		PS 3/4	PS 1/2	PS 1	PS 1/2
			PS 5/8		PS 2/5/6	
	PS 2	PS 4	PS 1/2		PS 3	
	PS 5	PS 3	PS 6		FD 5	FD 5
PS 3/5 FD 7			FD 1/2			
PS 4	PS 3/4	PS 1/2	PS 7	PS 4/5/6		PS 3/4
PS 6 FD 6	PS 5/6	PS 5/6		PS 2/3		PS 5/6
FD 1/3	FD 2/3	FD 2/3/5	FD 3	FD 1/2 3/4	FD 1/2	FD 2/3
FD 3/4/5	FD 4	FD 1/4/6	FD 4/5	FD 5/6	FD 3/6/7	FD 4/6
FD 3/4/7	FD 4	FD 6	FD 2	FD 6	FD 6/7	FD 5/6
	FD 5	FD 6	FD 5			
	FD 5				FD 6/7	

Key

UT   Understanding the text

PS   Producing the scene

FD   Further development

Further Reading

The following plays are suggested not because they fit indisputedly into the categories but because they are all suitable for reading in full or in part at the same level as Drama Sampler, and could be tackled in some of the ways suggested in this book.

Sad

Zoo Story,   E. Albee, Penguin
Killed,   Belgrade TIE, Amber Lane
Mother Courage,   B. Brecht, Methuen
Woyzeck,   G. Büchner, Methuen
Master Harold and the Boys,   A. Fugard, Oxford University Press
Dusa, Stas, Fish and Vi,   P. Gems, Methuen
The Normal Heart,   L. Kramer, Methuen
The Widowing of Mrs Holroyd,   D.H. Lawrence, Heinemann
A View From the Bridge,   A. Miller, Penguin
A Day in the Death of Joe Egg,   P. Nichols, Faber
Cyrano de Bergerac,   E. Rostand, Hutchinson
Blood Brothers,   W. Russell, Methuen
Journey's End,   R.C. Sheriff, Heinemann
Of Mice and Men,   J. Steinbeck, Samuel French
Home,   D. Storey, Samuel French
The Glass Menagerie,   T. Williams, Penguin

Strange

The Great American Dream,   E. Albee, Penguin
Endgame,   S. Beckett, Faber
Waiting for Godot,   S. Beckett, Faber
Gum and Goo,   H. Brenton, Methuen
Little Murders,   J. Feifer, Penguin
The Balcony,   J. Genet, Faber
Amadee, or, How to Get Rid Of It,   E. Ionesco, Penguin
Rhinoceros, The Chairs and The Lesson,   E. Ionesco, Penguin
The Ubu Plays,   A. Jarry, Methuen

Salonika,   L. Page, Methuen
The Caretaker,   H. Pinter, Methuen
The Lovers,   H. Pinter, Methuen
In Camera,   J.P. Sartre, Penguin
A Resounding Tinkle,   N.F. Simpson, Samuel French
Marat,   P. Weiss, Calder & Boyers

Angry

Antigone,   J. Anouilh, Methuen
Live Like Pigs,   J. Arden, Penguin
Sergeant Musgrave's Dance,   J. Arden, Methuen
The Biko Inquest,   Blair & Fenton, Collins
Saved,   E. Bond, Methuen
Light Shining in Buckinghamshire,   C. Churchill, Methuen
The Skin Game,   J. Galsworthy, Pan
Through the Night,   T. Griffiths, Faber
Savages,   C. Hampton, Faber
An Enemy of the People,   H. Ibsen, Methuen
The Crucible,   A. Miller, Penguin
Animal Farm,   G. Orwell, Metheun
Look Back in Anger,   J. Osborne, Faber
City Sugar,   S. Poliakoff, Methuen
Chips With Everything,   A. Wesker, Penguin

Funny

The Norman Conquests,   A.Ayckbourn, Penguin
The Resistable Rise of Arturo Ui,   B. Brecht, Methuen
The Way of the World,   W. Congreve, Penguin
Trumpets and Raspberries,   D. Fo, Pluto
The Fire Raisers,   M. Frisch, Methuen
The Government Inspector,   N. Gogol, Methuen
She Stoops to Conquer,   O. Goldsmith, Samuel French
Little Malcolm & His Struggle Against the Eunuchs,   D. Halliwell, Faber
The Bald Prima Donna,   E. Ionesco, Calder and Boyers
A Day in the Death of Joe Egg,   P. Nichols, Faber
The Erpingham Camp,   J. Orton, Methuen
Teahouse of the August Moon,   J. Patrick, Heinemann Educational Books
Black Comedy,   P. Shaffer, Samuel French

School for Scandal, R.B. Sheridan, Penguin
One Way Pendulum, N.F. Simpson, Faber
The Real Inspector Hound, T. Stoppard, Faber
Billy Liar, K. Waterhouse, Samuel French

Warm

Lives Worth Living, Belgrade TIE, Methuen
Hiawatha, P. Bogdanovitz, Methuen
The Beggar's Opera, J. Gay, Everyman's Library, Dent
Forget-Me-Not Lane, P. Nichols, Faber
Frost at Midnight, A. Obey, Samuel French
Beauty and the Beast, L. Page, Methuen
The Magistrate, A.W. Pinero, Methuen
When We Are Married, J.B. Priestley, Heinemann
The Winslow Boy, T. Rattigan, Samuel French
P'Tang, Yang, Kipperbang, J. Rosenthal, Longman
The Secret Diary of Adrian Mole, S. Townsend, Methuen
Lent, M. Wilcox, Methuen
Our Day Out, W. Russell, Methuen

In addition to the plays listed for further reading, the following novels might be of particular interest in that they are all accessible enough to be used as the basis for work on improvisation and scripting.

Sad

The Waterfall Box, John Gordon
A Game of Soldiers, Jan Needle
Summer of My German Solder, Susanne Newton
Brother in the Land, Robert Swindle
Dead Birds Singing, Marc Talbot
The Color Purple, Alice Walker
Goldengrove, Jill Paton Walsh
Unleaving, Jill Paton Walsh
The Pigman, Paul Zindel

Strange

The Bumblebee Flies Away,   Robert Cormier
The Gift,   Peter Dickinson
Stranger With My Face,   Lois Duncan
Sweets From a Stranger,   Nicholas Fisk
Red Shift,   Alan Garner
The Tricksters,   Margaret Mahy
Break of Dark,   Robert Westall
The Scarecrows,   Robert Westall

Angry

The Plague Dogs,   Richard Adams
I Know Why the Caged Bird Sings,   Maya Angelou
The Writing on the Wall,   Lynn Reid Banks
Come to Mecca,   Farrukh Dhondy
The Damned,   Linday Hoy
Your Friend Rebecca,   Linda Hoy
A Sense of Shame,   Jan Needle
Talking in Whispers,   James Watson

Funny

The Hitch Hikers Guide to the Galaxy,   Douglas Adams
Kill – a – Louse Week,   Susan Gregory
Freaky Friday,   Mary Rodgers
Harry's Mad,   Dick King Smith
Zac,   Frances Thomas
Tunes for a Small Harmonica,   Barbara Wersba

Warm

The Fox in Winter,   John Branfield
Goodnight Mr Tom,   Michelle Magorian
Catalogue of the Universe,   Margaret Mahy
Mrs Frisbee and the Rats of Nimh,   Robert C. O'Brien
Bridge to Terabithia,   Katherine Paterson